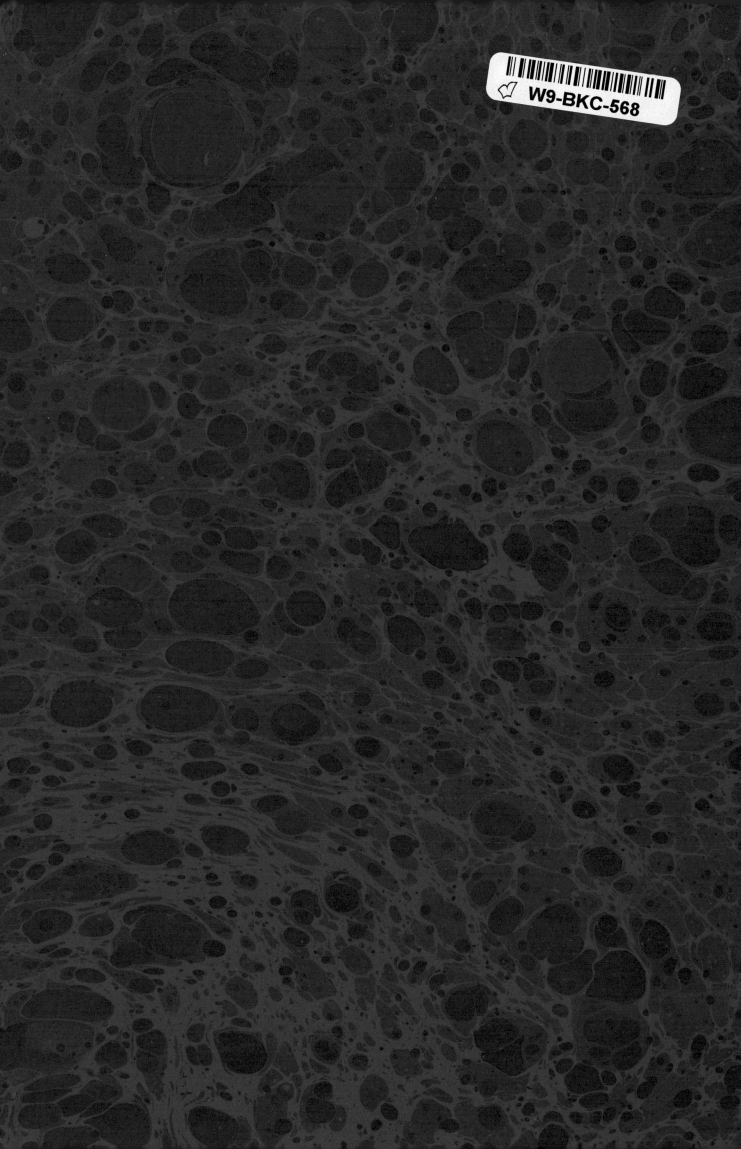

The Enchanted World
SPELLS AND BINDINGS

The Enchanted World

SPELLS AND BINDINGS

by the Editors of Time-Life Books

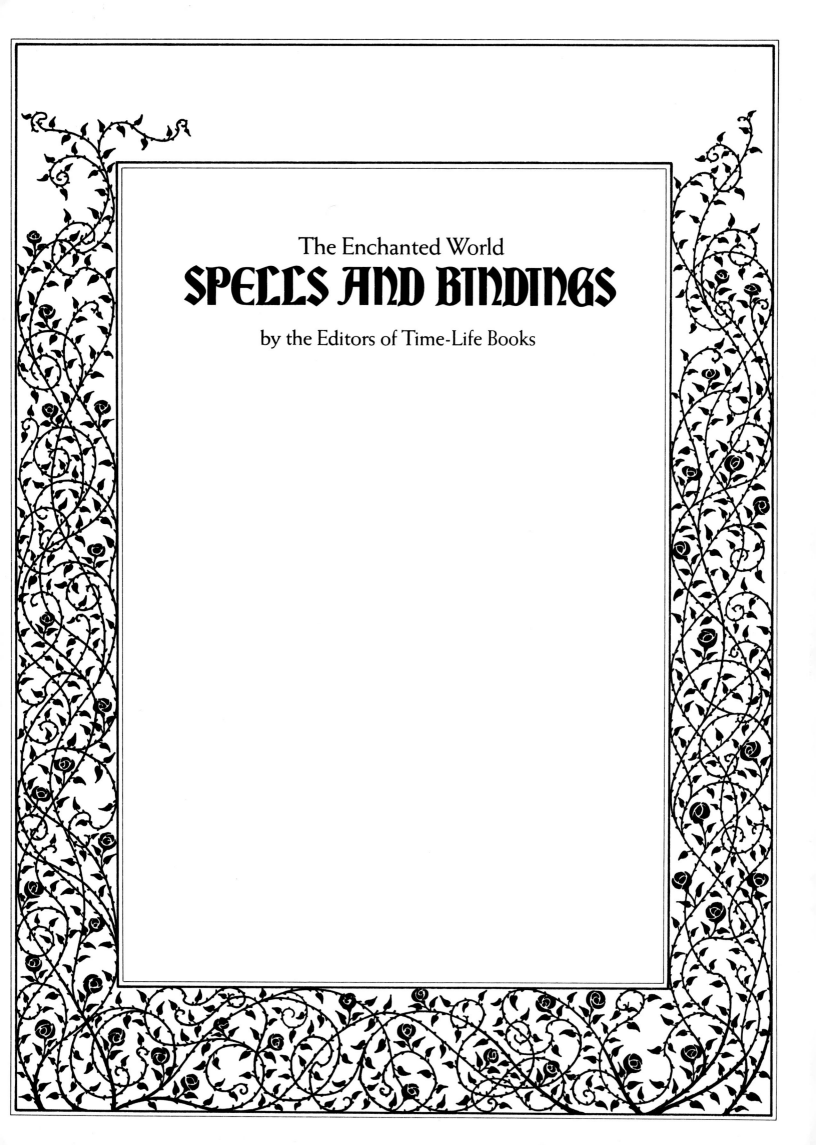

The Content

Time-Life Books · Alexandria, Virginia

Chapter One

W

Double-Edged Power

Who could have foretold the passion of Isolt the Fair and Tristram? When first they met, the Irish Princess was grieving her uncle's death in battle. Tristram, a British knight, was the uncle's slayer and therefore the enemy of Isolt and all her kin. But these two lived in troubled times, when the age of Arthur of Britain was drawing to a close and men and women were especially vulnerable to the forces of magic that still existed everywhere in the world. Magic would weave Tristram and Isolt a difficult fate indeed.

Tristram's very birth was bleak. It killed his mother. With her last breath, she gave him his name, which meant "the sorrowfully born child."

Sorrowfully born or not, he was the son of the King of Lyonnesse, a land that lay at the tip of Cornwall and, like the many other petty kingdoms scattered across the British Isles, paid fealty to Arthur. The child was given training worthy of a princeling. When he was old enough, he was sent to France to learn the language of the courtiers and the skills of war. He became a graceful harper and a fine hunter. By the time he was eighteen years old, he had grown into his full strength, and he traveled to the court of his uncle, King Mark of Cornwall, to gain his knighthood.

Skulking in the windy, seagirt fortress of Tintagel, the Cornish King had need of a valiant knight, as Tristram knew. Some time before, Mark had vaingloriously refused to send the annual tribute Cornwall customarily paid to Ireland. The Irish King dispatched his wife's brother, Marhaus by name, to present Mark with a simple choice: either pay the tribute or assign a champion to meet Marhaus in single combat and thus decide the issue. Marhaus encamped on an offshore island, waiting for the answer to his challenge. It was slow in coming. None of Mark's men wished to meet Marhaus on the field.

Tristram, however, was greedy for honor, and he asked to serve as King Mark's champion. Thus, on a morning in early spring, having been knighted by Mark, he sailed to the island. Marhaus—forewarned by Mark's herald—awaited him. Already mounted, with his spear held upright in a steady hand and his shield slung across his shoulder, Marhaus watched without expression while Tristram's men landed his horse and armed the fledgling knight.

In moments, the ritual of trial by arms began. Tristram and Marhaus shouted their challenges. Then, with lances leveled and shields across their bodies, they galloped at each other. The impact of their meeting knocked horses as well as men to the ground. Tristram, streaming blood from a wound made by Marhaus' lance, lurched to his feet and drew his sword.

The two knights circled, moving slowly under the weight of mail, shield and helmet, squinting through narrow slits in the visors that masked their faces. They slashed at each other again and again with their heavy broadswords. The blades clanged together or slammed against the leather shields, doing no damage. Then the men grappled, mailed chest to mailed chest, grunting viciously.

Marhaus was the more skilled, but Tristram was the younger. The Irish knight stumbled as his strength flagged. He recovered quickly and raised his sword in time to block the murderous arc of Tristram's blade. Again they grappled, Marhaus' breath coming in hoarse gasps. His legs buckled, and he sprawled on the ground. Down whistled Tristram's broadsword. The blade drove through Marhaus' helmet and deep into his brain, sending up a spray of blood and tissue. So ferocious was the stroke that the steel cracked, and when Tristram wrenched the sword away, a shard remained in Marhaus' head.

That battle was the youthful knight's first step on the road that led to Isolt and to dishonor. The Irish company sailed for home, taking their fallen champion with them. In Cornwall, Tristram languished: Marhaus' lance had been envenomed. The wound in the young man's side would not heal, and as it drained, Tristram's strength ebbed with it. The Cornish herbwives muttered over him, but they could not help. They told King Mark that the poisoned wound could be cured only in Ireland, where the poison had been made. And they specified that the physician should be Isolt, the niece of Marhaus and daughter of King Agwisance of Ireland. Her mother was a fairy, it was said, and perhaps because of this, the maiden had great powers of healing in her hands.

Heeding this advice, Mark sent the invalid to Ireland in the care of his squire, warning both the young knight and his servant not to reveal Tristram's name: The Irish were unlikely to welcome the man who had killed their champion. Some weeks later, on a sparkling May morning, Tristram lay on a litter in the courtyard of King Agwisance's fortress high above the Irish Sea. His big frame was gaunt and wasted; his flesh was gray, and his hair was matted from the sweat of his fevers. But his French schooling served him well. When Isolt appeared beside her father, gazing at Tristram curiously from a tower window, he sat up, took his harp from his squire's hands and played a lilting melody, fine enough to impress even the Irish, who were famed for their music. It was a splendidly gallant gesture. Tristram entered King Agwisance's hall not as a supplicant but as a guest. He said that his name was "Tramtrist of Lyonnesse" and that he had been wounded in a duel over a woman.

During the weeks that followed, Tristram and Isolt were much together. At first he was too weak to leave the chamber he was given, and Isolt spent hours there,

*Love was foreign to King Mark of Cornwall, but magic might have wedded his heart
to Isolt the Fair of Ireland—had not the impassioning spell gone amiss in Isolt's hands.*

bathing his wound and watching beside him through his fever-ridden nights. Then Tristram began to mend, and his songs floated through the corridors of the fortress, where Agwisance and his people still mourned Marhaus' death.

So sweet was Tristram's singing, so merry his nature and pleasant his glance that the Irish were charmed, Isolt not least. His gallantry saved him when his deception was revealed by the Irish Queen, who discovered that the shard she had carefully drawn from Marhaus' brain fitted the blade of Tristram's sword. In spite of her demands, Agwisance refused to take vengeance. He said merely that the fight had been an honorable one, and he sent Tristram out of the country for his own safety.

Isolt wept to see him go; naïvely, she gave him a ring and called him her true knight.

Tristram returned to King Mark healthy and vigorous and full of tales of Isolt's beauty. He entered enthusiastically into the hunts and tournaments that occupied the men of the Cornish court, and his admiration for the Irish Princess did not deter him from dalliance. Quite the contrary; within weeks of his return he successfully campaigned for the affections of the wife of a Cornish knight named Segwarides.

The affair pleased no one but the two principals. Segwarides naturally was unhappy. He made the mistake of fighting with Tristram in his wife's name, and got for his pains a belly wound that kept him an invalid for months. King Mark also was angry: The old man desired Segwarides' wife himself and might have had his way with that light lady except for Tristram.

But Mark, who was known as "King Fox" because of his slyness, did not challenge his nephew openly. Disguised in plain armor and accompanied by two men, he ambushed Tristram one night as the young man rode to a tryst. Tristram knocked all three men unconscious. Without stopping to unlace their helmets and identify them, he went on about his business.

*A*fter that humiliation, hatred settled in Mark's sour soul. Outwardly, he was courteous. He had no desire for a second defeat. And Tristram's fame had spread as far as the Round Table at Camelot, where Arthur, the High King, ruled. It was beginning to be said that among British knights, Tristram was second in valor only to Lancelot. Killing such a man would bring only shame to Cornwall.

Mark brooded for a while, then conceived a scheme to rid himself of his competitor. "Grant me a boon," he said to Tristram, who promptly offered anything in his power. Mark was his uncle and the man who had knighted him, and honor demanded unquestioning loyalty in return. Besides, the chance of adventure did much to alleviate the idleness of peacetime.

"Bring me Isolt of Ireland for a wife."

This was a hard task indeed. King Agwisance surely would be unwilling to give Isolt to Mark: She was his rose, a maiden just out of girlhood, whereas Mark was old, devious and no friend to Ireland. Very likely, reasoned Mark, the Irish King would have the young knight killed.

It happened, for reasons not important to the story, that Agwisance was then at King Arthur's fortress, facing a charge against his honor. To Camelot, Tristram therefore journeyed; he sought out Agwisance and offered to defend his name in single combat, provided that Agwisance swear his innocence of the charge and also promise whatever reasonable reward Tristram asked. Agwisance agreed.

Tristram fought for him and won both the battle and the Irish King's gratitude. Together, the two men then sailed to Ireland. Tristram was welcomed grandly. Great fires blazed in Agwisance's hall, and the King smiled to see how Isolt gazed with shining eyes at the fine young knight. One evening, in the presence of the whole court, Agwisance reminded Tristram that he had not yet named his reward.

"Now is the time, then," Tristram said.

He hesitated and cleared his throat. "I ask that you give me Isolt the Fair, not for myself, but as a bride for Mark of Cornwall. I have promised to bring her to him."

A stricken silence followed. So quiet was the hall that the rustling of women's robes was clearly audible as the Queen and her women gathered protectively around Isolt, shielding her from view. But neither man looked in the women's direction.

At last, Agwisance said heavily, "I have given my word to you. But I would give all my lands that you and not King Mark should wed my daughter."

"Sir," Tristram replied, "Isolt the Fair is a fine maiden, and you honor me in offering her. But I cannot take the offer. I would be false to my promise to my King. Shame would follow me forever."

This was true, and Agwisance knew it. Just as Agwisance had given Tristram his word and must keep it, Tristram had given Mark his word and must keep it.

"Isolt is yours, then," said King Agwisance. "If you will not marry her, then wed her to King Mark."

In the weeks that followed, Tristram saw little of the Princess who had become his charge, and what he saw did not seem promising. Isolt was obedient to her father's will: She had only bowed her head when she heard her father's words, but she was pale as a wraith and silent.

Her mother watched her closely and took care that the bride was well provided for. The mules that daily plodded from fortress to harbor were laden with treasures to please a maiden far from home—tunics of satin in the bright colors the Irish loved, mantles of otter and seal, veils of linen as sheer as mist, armlets and crescent-shaped collars of worked gold, brooches of bronze, hollow golden spheres to swing from the ends of the Princess's long braids.

Nothing was forgotten. Isolt's mother sent bronze mirrors in the train, as well as combs of creamy horn. She herself, with her fairy's skill, blended oils and herbs for bathing and sealed them in little ivory pots. And, anxious for her daughter's success with the old King Mark, she sent another, secret confection of her own—a sparkling wine as clear as moonlight, encased in a golden flagon. She put the liquid in the charge of Isolt's waiting woman and told her to guard its secret with her life. The wine was enchanted. Served to Mark and Isolt on their wedding night, it would bind them as lovers forever.

Finally, on a fine autumn morning, all was ready. The little ship that Agwisance provided—a square-sailed vessel called a *knarr*, adorned with painted castles fore and aft and gleaming with gilt—sped away from the Irish shore. On the deck, Isolt, the reluctant bride, sat with her hands folded in her lap. She spoke to no one, except to send her waiting woman below. Oblivious of the bustlings of the crew and the courteous comments of Tristram, she looked westward until the cliffs of Ireland faded from view.

Tristram was discomfited by her sadness and sat down beside her. He told her about Cornwall, and about the splendors of Tintagel, high on its promontory, but Isolt made no response. He mentioned King Mark, but all the answer he got was a

The means of enchantment were perilous in the hands of mortals. All
unknowing, Tristram and Isolt drank a fairy-made wine intended for other lips.
The draught bound them together for the term of their lives and even beyond.

sidelong glance from the Princess. A faint flush stained her cheeks.

Irritated, Tristram tried another tack. "Lady," he said, as one might speak to a sullen child, "here is a good thing to please you, left lying about by your waiting woman; it is fine wine, to speed your journey along." He offered the golden flagon.

Isolt shook her head.

Patiently, Tristram poured out the wine. A heady scent curled up from the cup he held, a compound of flowers and rich earth and wood smoke and darker things, familiar but unidentifiable. "See how clear it is. I will drink first, to your good fortune," he said, and drank.

He lowered the cup when he had drunk, and he stared down at the woman, at the shadow of her lashes on her cheek, at the down along the fine-drawn bone and at the delicate scrollwork of the ear, revealed when the wind lifted her hair. So profound was his stillness that Isolt looked up.

Rising, he pulled Isolt to her feet and placed the wine cup in her hands. "Drink, Isolt," said Tristram.

That wine – made with the aid of fairy arts, entrusted to a careless mortal woman, and drunk unknowingly – altered Tristram's and Isolt's lives. His carefree admiration and her innocent devotion were translated by magic into passion. Unlike most mortal loves, it never faded into comfortable affection. It distorted Tristram's path through the world; he became not only one born of sorrow but one who lived in sorrow. It distorted sunny Isolt's path no less profoundly, and it distorted the paths of those around them.

The accounts that exist of Tristram and Isolt vary widely, but in all of them it is clear that the code of honor governing human behavior was immediately weakened. They became lovers on shipboard, and they were happy beyond the power of words to describe. Still, they tried to maintain at least the outward form of right behavior. When they reached Cornwall, Isolt married King Mark in a ceremony of some splendor; Tristram distinguished himself at the wedding tournaments.

They continued, however, as lovers, and it was inevitable that they be caught. The glance too long held, the hands that brushed together too often were enough to rouse King Mark's suspicion. That suspicion was confirmed when a nephew of the King's saw the pair together one day in Isolt's apartments. Raging, Mark charged into his wife's chamber and found Tristram. He threatened the young knight with a sword. Tristram seized the weapon and beat the King with the flat of its blade, "so that," in the contemptuous words of one chronicler, "he made him fall on his nose." Tristram's prowess in battle – and

Mark's councilors, who feared that, if dismissed, the young knight would join Arthur's company and turn the High King against Cornwall – persuaded Mark to maintain a semblance of cordiality.

This unlovely triangle continued for many years, amid the panoply of feast and tournament, quest and duel that marked the court life of the day. Sometimes Mark had Tristram imprisoned; sometimes he hid Isolt in secret places, far from her lover's arms. But the two always found each other again. For a time, Tristram was exiled to Brittany, and there he married a Princess of that land, also named Isolt. He left her instantly when he received a despairing letter from Isolt the Fair.

Sometimes, indeed, the three were reconciled – once by order of King Arthur – and a kind of uneasy peace prevailed for a while. But Mark could not long tolerate the cuckold's horns. It was said that he found Tristram sitting in Isolt's chamber and playing the harp for her, and that he stabbed his rival with a poisoned spear. Isolt nursed her lover day after day, but he faded before her eyes as the poison burned and shriveled him. Finally he died, having dwindled to a wasted memory of the young warrior she had loved.

Thus the magic lost its hold on him. Isolt lingered after her lover for some days, but she could not long survive Tristram; it was his love, she said, that had given her life. She was found dead one morning, stretched across his bier. They were buried at Tintagel in separate graves. Yet even death did not completely undo the power of the enchantment. Trees grew from the graves and twined together, finding and sustaining union long after the lovers' bodies had turned to dust. As for Mark, it was told either that one of his knights killed him to avenge Tristram or that he died imprisoned for his crime.

Thus were three lives twisted by magic gone awry. Isolt and Tristram had some joy in it: Poets said their moments together, even after many years, blazed with the fires of spring and that the fairy wine gave them delight other mortals only dreamed of. But their love rent the fragile fabric of order that defined their world. The magic, fluid and inchoate, was antithetical to that order. Its ancient force was too great for human souls to contain and too powerful to trust to human hands. Isolt's mother herself had said that her wine held both love and death.

In her curious statement lay an explanation difficult for mortals to comprehend. The scraps and shreds of magic that lingered on into the age of Arthur and beyond were relics of the dawn of time, when the riot of creation had not settled into the stable patterns that humans depended upon. The forces of enchantment were paradoxical to human minds. In themselves neither good nor evil, they had the potential for both good and evil, like the Irish Queen's love-engendering wine.

A number of different beings – survivors of the early ages of the earth – wielded magic power. They might be called fairies in England; Twlwyth Teg – or "the Fair Family" – in Wales; or *alfar*, which meant "elves," in Scandinavia. Once masters of the world, they were now retreating before the new race, humanity. Their kingdoms were beneath the sea or under the ground or hidden among the clouds or simply invisible. Some of these beings, however, walked among men and women and even married them, as Isolt's mother did.

The human attitude toward the forces of the first world was full of doubt and conflict. On the one hand, marvels seemed to flow from magic; on the other, magic held the dangers of the unknown and was therefore to be feared.

Usually, however, the evidence of the marvels was enough to override the fear. These centuries were hard ones. Britain, for instance, was divided into a number of intermittently hostile kingdoms and was a favorite target of sea raiders from the European mainland. The countryside thus was frequently laid waste as rival armies or freebooting marauders swept across. Even in times of peace, starvation or disease cut many lives short, and backbreaking labor hastened the descent into old age. Most people, poorly dressed and ill shod, lived in flimsy, dirt-floored dwellings of wood or lath and plaster. Given such hardships, it heartened men and women to learn that wishes could indeed come true.

People liked, for instance, to hear the Greek tale of Pygmalion. This sculptor had no love for women, it was thought. At least no Greek woman pleased him. Solitary and sullen, he kept to his workshop.

But in his sun-washed courtyard, under the blue Greek sky, Pygmalion created the object of his dreams. He had acquired a tusk of perfect ivory, and he sculpted it

Once wishes came true: Finding women flawed,
the Greek sculptor Pygmalion carved an ivory
maiden, fair but cold and still. He wished her living . . .

into a figure. A woman—the image, the ancients said, of love itself—emerged from the gleaming bone. Her hair curled in the finest of tendrils, her face was that of a maiden goddess, and her body curved more sweetly than any woman's ever had. Pygmalion had made a wonder.

And so he thought it. He idolized this product of his artist's hands. He brought the figure flowers and adorned it with jewels. He whispered his love, and waited for answers that did not come. The figure returned his gaze with blank ivory eyes.

He prayed to his gods, the storytellers said, and at last the very force of his love stirred the ivory to life. The sculptor stroked it, and the cool bone warmed and softened in his hand. Under his fingers, he felt a pulse begin to throb. With each caress, rosy shadows bloomed in the pale flesh. The lips trembled into a smile and, stepping from her pedestal, Pygmalion's statue entered his arms. It was a tale with the happiest of endings: The woman lived with Pygmalion all his life and bore his children. Pygmalion, it seemed, had found a way to channel the life forces that flowed through the universe. He had given soul to a graven image.

Pygmalion's tale was not unique. Long before his time, Egyptians told of magicians who made figurines of workers—carpenters and stonecutters, painters and calligraphers—and then caused them to breathe and live. These creations served, it was said, to swell the vast armies of laborers who built the pyramids of the pharaohs. Much later, the Swedes described puppets whose souls could be enkindled by a drop of human blood. And the Japanese said that dolls, played with by affectionate generations of children, acquired souls and served as protectors of their human households.

The old life force of enchantment manifested itself in many other ways, flowing through commonplace objects and making those objects the servants of humankind. For the hungry, there was food. The British told wistful tales of a simple wooden table that, when commanded, obediently spread itself with loaves of bread, great wheels of cheese and jugs of beer. Among the French, this cornucopia was said to be contained in a napkin, which could be placed on any table and ordered to produce a meal. The Italians and the Irish believed that the magic storehouse was an apparently empty linen sack.

For the adventurous, there were articles to be had that served as aid and protection: enchanted boots that carried the wearer seven leagues with each step; cloaks and rings that conferred invisibility; and magic clothing, like the hood of the Irish warrior Finn Mac Cumal, which could change Finn's shape to that of a hound or deer and back again, as he wished.

Some magical objects were said to make fighting men invulnerable, and a knight going into single combat during the Middle Ages was required to swear that he carried no such aid. A few such enchanted tools of war worked on a truly grand scale. It was said in Scotland, for example, that the MacLeod clan had a magic banner that, when waved, called forth a host to defeat MacLeod enemies. It could be used only

. . . and she was given life. Some said the goddess
Aphrodite heard Pygmalion's plea and animated
the ivory figure with her own loving touch.

On the wings of wishes

In bygone days, objects charged with
magic were widespread in the world
and could even be bought: Many
served only as trinkets in the treasuries
of rich lords. Indian storytellers, for
instance, chronicled the adventures of
three Princes who lived in the northern mountains. These Princes were
brothers and rivals for the same young
woman; to decide the issue fairly, the
Sultan who was her guardian sent the
men on quests. Each was to travel for a
year and return with a wonder. He
who brought the finest offering would
have the Princess for his own.

One brother, called Husayn, journeyed south to the low plain that lay
beside the Arabian Sea. He searched
the crowded bazaars of the city of Vi-
jayanagar and at length found a treasure indeed. It was a splendid carpet,
scarlet in color, laced with blue
threads and strands of gold. Power
had been woven into the fabric, for
the carpet would carry its owner where
he wished. Husayn paid forty thou-
sand gold pieces for it.

When it was his, Husayn sat upon
the rug and gave a command, and the
carpet trembled into life. It rose above
the turbaned heads of the merchants,
above the city roofs shimmering in the
heat, above the green and steaming
plain, into the clear heights among the
clouds. Rippling and fluttering, riding
the air, the carpet carried Husayn
north to his mountains, where he met
his brothers and the Sultan.

Husayn's brothers had found
wonders as well. One had discovered a
tube of ivory; whoever gazed through
it would see any event he wished, far
or near. The offering of the other
brother was a humble apple – but its
flesh restored life to the ailing.

The incomparable treasures were
evenly matched. In the end, the hand
of the maiden was won, simply
enough, by an archery contest among
the brothers. Husayn lost; he retired
to the wilds to live as a hermit. As for
the carpet, the ivory tube and the apple, they disappeared into the Sultan's
strong room, never to be seen again.

in extremity, however, and only at intervals of a year and a day, or else the MacLeod land and livestock would become barren. The banner had been given to an early Crusading MacLeod by a water fairy, and it was kept for centuries in the castle that was the laird's seat, at the head of Loch Dunvegan on the Isle of Skye.

Most enticing of all, there was gold to be had for those lucky few who knew where to look. According to the British, certain mules dropped golden ingots; in Austria, the animal was a nanny goat; in Ireland, a hen that laid golden eggs.

Such magical objects and creatures were not uncommon once, but the approach to them required the greatest caution. All these relics of elder magics were bound and protected in ways that men and women no longer understood. Sometimes the objects were watched by fierce and ancient guardians, terrifying to behold. Sometimes they were shrouded in spells that could be penetrated only by complex rituals. In dealing with the artifacts of magic, the consequences of mistaken action, of a careless word or any other offense against guardian or ritual, could be disastrous. Of the hundreds of accounts that show the perils, one from Germany will suffice:

The island of Rügen, in the Baltic Sea off the north coast of Pomerania, was known to be haunted by spirits from the long-forgotten past. Once it had been the home of the Teutonic goddess Nerthus, and long after her cult had been abandoned, her shade walked the forests near the mountain that was her throne, luring unwary wanderers into the depths of a lake. She demanded one human soul a year, people said. But Nerthus was not the only elder spirit of Rügen. Near the little market town of Garz dwelled another, an ancient chieftain who had ruled the region. The ruins of his stone fortress and its ring of earthworks lay beside a lake near the town; it seemed that the place had been destroyed by Christians seeking to root out the old faith. But that chieftain was no ordinary being, and he lived on in many guises. Sometimes he appeared at night in warrior's form, helmeted in gold and riding a gray horse; sometimes he was seen as a vicious black dog; sometimes as an aged man wearing a black fur cap.

In all his manifestations, he served as watchman for his castle's ruins, under which was buried his barbaric hoard—his weapons, his jewels and, above all, his gold. The villagers said that he would freely give the treasure to the maiden who dared to approach him, if she performed a certain ceremonial, and if she was chaste.

Eventually, a maiden tried, and not primarily for gold. She was the daughter of a lord whose estate lay near Garz; she had been accused by envious servants of unchastity, and she dared the chieftain's stronghold in order to prove her virtue.

In every respect, she followed the ritual as it was prescribed. She appeared alone near the lake at the time ordained: at midnight on Midsummer Eve. Near the crumbled earthworks she paused to remove her veil and gold circlet, her tunic and her underdress. She laid them in the damp grass, then, pale as moonlight, walked into the chieftain's precincts,

Summoning a spirit servant

Many elder beings lurked among humans once. Arabia, for example, was the home of a spirit-race called the jinn. Said to be the most ancient of creatures, born of fire, they dwelled in hiding, but they could be summoned to provide treasure, as a boy named Aladdin discovered.

He was the orphan of a poor tailor and lived in a bazaar, supporting himself and his mother in the way street urchins did then: picking rags, begging, doing errands. It happened that a magician sent Aladdin after a treasure – an oil lamp, battered, blackened and wickless – that was hidden away in a small desert cave. Aladdin took the commission eagerly, but he kept the lamp for himself, thinking that it might be sold for food.

His mother sighed when she saw the humble object, but she polished it diligently, to brighten it for selling. The rubbing was a summons. Flame leaped from the lamp, and from the fire arose a jinni, blue as the light that formed it. It saluted the boy and called him master. Aladdin asked for food. With a flick of his massive hand, the jinni summoned a banquet, served in vessels of silver and gold. Aladdin ate his fill, then sold the cups and plates for cash. But profit was easier to come by than that, as the boy soon learned. Whatever Aladdin wanted, he had only to request. The spirit gave the youth the clothes and slaves and jewels of a prince. When Aladdin's heart turned toward a Sultan's daughter, the jinni protected him in the maze of court intrigue, so that he won the maiden and became Prince indeed. When Aladdin fought the wars of the Sultan, the jinni provided horses and soldiers. And in the end, thanks to the magic of the lamp and his own clever use of it, the bazaar boy became first the Sultan's heir, then Sultan himself. It was said, moreover, that his rule was a wise one.

climbed the cold stones of the fortress wall, and walked among the ruins backward, never looking over her shoulder.

An hour passed. Then, as she backed through a courtyard, an opening appeared at her feet. Candlelight glowed in the gap, revealing the steps of a winding stair. Down the stair she trod, following it into the earth until she came to a rock vault.

Torches gleamed there, throwing crazy shadows on the sweating walls. The floor was strewn with gold—goblets and drinking horns, coins so old that their markings were gone. In the midst of the treasure stood an aged man, gray as the stones of his vault, gray as the dead. He stared at the maid, his face crinkling with amusement.

"Well, mortal," he said, "you have gained the treasure from me. Take a coin and leave, if you can. My servants will follow with the rest."

He did not remind her of the rest of the ritual, but she knew what it was. She must not speak here. She must not look behind her when she left, for mortal eyes were forbidden to see the activities of this world.

Without a word, she took a coin. She turned and began to mount the stair. Although she had seen no servants, she heard at her back the clink of metal and rustlings and scurryings, as if small, clawed creatures scuttled behind her.

Up the stairs she went, clutching the coin and shivering in the chill. She kept her eyes fixed straight ahead. Far above, at the door that crowned the stair, summer stars glimmered.

Scratches and clicks—the footsteps of the treasure-laden servants—came closer; small air currents curled and whispered at her feet. Something grazed her ankle. With a start, she glanced back into the pit.

What she saw was never known. With a roar that echoed across the waters of the lake below the fortress, a stone slab crashed down over the doorway to freedom, trapping the maiden forever in the lair of the old chieftain.

The villagers of Garz found her clothing the next morning. Although her father searched, he could not find the door that led to the vault. He and generations of his descendants, however, heard at night the thin, despairing wails of this young woman, who had dared a place of enchantment and broken its law.

It was always that way. The enchantment that lingered in the world of humankind offered nothing simply. Like the fairy wine, compounded of both love and death, the beings and objects and rituals of the elder ages of the earth were paradoxes. They promised both infinite pleasure and infinite sorrow; the end depended on the way men and women used them.

But the things of the elder ages were foreign now—songs whose words were more than half-forgotten. Many mortals failed as the maiden of Rügen failed: They could not keep in key, and the music ended in discord. So humans viewed the wonders with both longing and suspicion.

This ambivalence pervades the chronicles of Wales. Remote and free from invaders for many centuries, Wales seemed to keep its magic longer than most places. A sense of enchantment lingered in its valleys and hovered in its forests. In that rough country, the borders between mortals and the fairy races were membranous and readily crossed. A man might set out on a hunt and find himself in a region where animals could talk. He might sail from the Welsh shore in a ship and fetch up not where he intended but on an island crowned by castles of glass and peopled by beings who were no more than voices.

In the southwest of Wales once lived a Prince who was especially familiar with enchantment. His name was Pwyll, and he ruled Dyfed, a realm of seven cantrefs — seven regions of a hundred farms or hamlets each — and of much land in between. In his youth he fought among the people of the other worlds of Wales; for his valor in these exploits, he sometimes was called Head of Annwfn — or "not world" — rather than Prince of Dyfed.

Pwyll's principal court was at Narberth, in the south of his lands. Here he dwelled in a high, thatched hall, well guarded by ditches and wooden ramparts. A dense forest surrounded the stronghold, and among the trees, suggestions of Faerie were to be seen — great grass-covered mounds that some said were the funeral barrows of old chieftains and some said were the gates to kingdoms that lay beneath the earth. The Welsh believed that a person who stood on one of the mounds either would be terribly wounded or would witness enchantment. The double-edged character was typical of magic, and most people avoided the mounds. But Pwyll, after a night of feasting, once announced that he would stand upon a knoll and take what chance gave him.

It gave a wonder. Among the beech trees surrounding the mound appeared a glimmer of gold, sometimes flashing in the shafts of light that filtered through the canopy of leaves, sometimes fading into shadow. It took shape at last as a woman. She rode a white horse, and she was clothed in a cloak and gown of gold so luminous that she seemed to wear the sun itself for a garment. Her face, within its aureole of pale hair, was grave and quiet; she had no glance to spare for the Welsh Prince or the companions who watched nearby. She rode past at a steady trot and vanished from view.

Pwyll sent a page after her, but the boy soon returned. The woman, he said, had neither speeded nor slackened her horse's pace, but he could not catch her, no matter how he urged his horse. Pwyll listened closely. Then he leaped from the mound and led his companions home.

wyll waited alone at the place the next afternoon, and again the woman appeared among the trees. This time Pwyll himself, mounted on his charger, followed her. Like the page, he could not catch her. His horse trotted at the same pace as hers, then increased its speed, but the space between them remained the same. At length, when his horse's flanks were flecked with foam, Pwyll halted.

"Maiden," he called. "For the sake of him you love, halt and speak with me."

She halted and brought her horse's head around. When she did, it seemed that there had been no distance between them. The horses stood flank to flank.

"I halt, and willingly," the maiden said.

In the wild country of Wales, the Fairy Princess Rhiannon sought the love
of a mortal, Prince Pwyll. Wreathed in the light of her own world, she appeared before
him, riding a white horse. He followed her and, in the end, took her for his wife.

With a smile at his tired mount, she added, "It would have been better for the horse if you had called before. It needed only a word to stop me."

"Why do you travel alone in this wood?" asked Pwyll.

"To find you, Prince."

"Who are you, and why do you seek me?"

"I am Rhiannon. I seek you for love."

Adventure had come upon him. This was a fairy woman and a powerful one. Her name meant "great queen." That she should leave her people for him was a grace beyond reckoning, and Pwyll accepted it, for the sight of the woman had struck him to the heart.

"I welcome you, lady," Pwyll said gravely. He reached across to take her reins, but Rhiannon smiled and shook her head.

"Return to me in a year and I shall welcome you," she said. She spurred the horse gently; it slipped through the trees, and in another moment, she had disappeared.

Yielding to the rule, although he did not understand it, Pwyll left the place. He bided his time for the requisite year, and when the day came, he took a troop of his own men, as was fitting for a prince on his wedding day, and rode to the mound where he had last seen Rhiannon.

She was there in her golden dress, riding her white horse. When she saw them, she wheeled her mount and gestured, and the men fell into line behind her.

They followed the fairy woman into the tangled depths of the wood. Where she guided her horse, a clear path opened; the trees sighed and bowed and parted before her and her mortal company, closing like a curtain behind the last man in the line. Pwyll's men noticed this and spoke anxiously among themselves, but Pwyll paid them no heed, seeing only Rhiannon.

Before long, the wood thinned out, and the party came to a broad clearing. Here a palace stood, one unlike any in the mortals' world. It had no fortifications: The fairy race had no need of walls and watchtowers. It was built not of the wood and thatch that formed Pwyll's own fortresses, but of silvery stone clustered in soaring spires, rising like a stand of enormous water reeds from the center of a glassy lake. As the wedding party entered the clearing, a flock of tiny scarlet birds tumbled up into the air above Rhiannon's head. At the sound of their liquid caroling, all fear left the mortal men.

After that came a time of feasting. The hall of Rhiannon's father was so high that the vaults of the ceiling appeared and disappeared in the flickering light of the fairy hearth fires. And Rhiannon's people were elusive, too. They were merry and welcoming, it is true. When they spoke to the mortals, they seemed to be men and women, although all of them shared the slender, gilded fairness of the Princess. But when they ceased to speak to Pwyll or his company, they seemed to fade; the silent members of that race gave the appearance of reflections in water, shimmering among the crowd. The air seemed full of faint echoes, as if unheard talk was going on.

It was said that at this feast there was a quarrel, that one of her own kind claimed Rhiannon, to try to keep her among her

people, and that by her powers she prevented him. Then she departed from her country with Pwyll and went into Wales as his Princess. They rode through the forest as before, and the trees opened before them and closed behind them until they came to the place of the green mound. There they halted, and Rhiannon gave a last look at the tangled wall of the forest.

"That wall will open to me no more," she said to Pwyll softly. But she did not seem grieved by the loss.

Rhiannon was welcomed by the people of Pwyll's court. Everyone knew that she was one of the Fair Family, but she had left her other-world self behind. She presided over the rustic fortress serenely, giving no sign of longing for the splendor of her former realm, and she seemed as solid and real as any mortal woman, if more beautiful. She was adept at weaving, and the cloth from her high loom was finer, perhaps, than that of other women. She would not touch the harps they had, but she sang when the harpers played, and her singing always had a note in it that seemed foreign to her listeners, an echo perhaps of the other world.

So Rhiannon was accepted by the people of the husband she had so strangely chosen. But it was a reserved acceptance at best. When two years had gone by and Rhiannon had still produced no heir for Pwyll, the question of her bloodline arose—as it had before—among the men who served as his guard and council. They asked him to put her away and take another wife. As they pointed out, he would not live forever, and a son of his body was needed to lead them.

The Prince understood this. He asked for one more year. At the end of that year, Rhiannon was delivered of a son. He was a fine child, as fair in coloring as his mother but as sturdily built as his father. He was shown to Pwyll's people in the great hall some hours after he was born, and they cheered him. There was relief in that cheer: Who knew what sort of child the fairy woman might have had?

The child, however, was the source of Rhiannon's sorrow. For some time after her lying-in, she kept to the women's quarters of the palace, as was the custom. Six waiting women stayed with her, to serve the mother and guard the child. Although these women were supposed to watch in turn through each night while Rhiannon slept and regained her strength, they failed in their duty. An evening came when, one by one, they nodded into sleep.

When they stirred in the small hours, the cradle was empty. The casement window above it rattled in the night wind. Beside the cradle, on a silk-covered pallet, Rhiannon lay motionless, sleeping as if caught in an enchantment.

The waiting women were petty creatures. All their fear of the outlander returned and, with it, fear for themselves. They had failed in watchfulness, and the punishment for the loss of the child might be their lives.

They had a natural scapegoat, however, in the sleeping Princess. Working in silence, they strangled one of the many staghounds that were allowed to roam freely through the fortress. They cut up

From the union of Pwyll and Rhiannon came a fair son. He vanished from
his cradle, stolen in the night by a being of the other world. But the people of
Pwyll's court charged Rhiannon, the fairy stranger, with murdering the boy.

A punishment was devised for the fairy: Wearing a horse collar,
Rhiannon guarded her husband's gate, confessing her story
to passersby and carrying them on her back like an animal.

the animal, smeared Rhiannon with the blood, and dropped some of the bloody bones on her pallet. Then they squatted around her and waited for the light.

The Princess awoke at last. Still half-asleep, she reached for her infant. When she touched the empty cradle, she sat up at once. She looked at the avid, frightened human faces that surrounded her and said, "Where is my boy?"

"Gone," replied one woman. "You have killed him, fairy woman. Only see the blood on you."

"Ladies, it is not true. Do not accuse me because you fear punishment. I will protect you." But the women would not have it. They would have dragged her to the Prince and council, but Rhiannon struck them away from her and walked proudly before them into Pwyll's hall.

The end of this was that fear of the Fair Family returned in full force. Although Rhiannon declared her innocence before her husband and his people, she could not produce her missing son. And all could see the blood that matted her shining hair. Faced with this mystery and with the anger of his council, Pwyll was weak and passive. He would not divorce his wife as they demanded, but he gave her to them to suffer what penance they chose.

"Lady," he pleaded at the end of that day. "Can you not lift whatever enchantment this is?"

"I left enchantment behind me, Pwyll, when I left my folk to come to you. It is you who must protect me."

But Pwyll only gestured helplessly.

The next day, his wife's punishment—bizarre-sounding, but not unknown in Celtic countries—began. All day long, bent under the weight of a heavy horse collar, Rhiannon was made to sit on a stone horse block that stood beside the principal gate of the fortress. She had to stop each passerby and tell of her supposed crime. And she had to offer to carry each one on her back to Pwyll's hall.

The punishment was to last for seven years. From the start, Rhiannon bore it without complaining. She had no choice, being among humans, with no one to defend her. In the dust and heat of summer, in the mud and cold of winter, the Princess from the palace of silver stone sat on the horse block. In a toneless voice, she recited her punishment to each person who passed and offered to carry that person on her back. But such was her fine-drawn beauty and her dignity that few took her offer. And word of the wretched punishment spread throughout Wales, carried on the lips of travelers.

In the fourth year, on an autumn day, three strangers on horseback appeared at the gate of Pwyll's fortress. One was a comely man, dressed in the fine woolen cloak and gleaming arm rings of a lord; one was a woman, clearly his lady; and one was a golden-haired boy.

Rhiannon rose to her feet beside the horse block. "Lord, for that I killed my only son, I am bidden to carry each one of you to the Prince's court on my back. That is the term of my punishment," she said.

The man shook his head and swung down from the saddle. "Princess," he said, "no one here will ride upon your back."

Through four winters, Rhiannon endured. But humans were kind as well as cruel:
Her son had been found far away; when the foster parents recognized the child as
Pwyll's, they returned him to the court and thus freed the fairy from her pillory.

"I will not," said his wife.

"Nor I," said the child, and he, too, dismounted. He held out to Rhiannon a short length of brocaded cloth. She took it from him, turning it over slowly in her hands. The cloth was of her own weaving. The boy smiled up at her, and his eyes were the eyes of his father, Pwyll.

Then the man, who was Teirnyon, lord of the province of Gwent in the east, set Rhiannon on his horse and led her, with her son walking beside, into Pwyll's hall.

The end of the account was this: Pwyll and all his people recognized the boy for who he was – Pwyll's son, and Rhiannon's. Rhiannon was restored to honor and to her place beside her husband, and if she felt anger over the humans' treatment of her, she said nothing.

But the story Teirnyon had to tell was a curious one, full of darkness. Four years before, on Beltane Eve, he had brought a mare into his fortress in Gwent, with the intention of protecting her. The mare was in labor; the foals she had dropped in previous years had all disappeared in the night, and Teirnyon had no intention of losing this one. The mare dropped her foal. It was a fine one, and as it lurched, trembling, to its feet, an enormous clawed arm reached through a window of the chamber and grasped the foal by its mane. Teirnyon, a brave man, seized his broadsword and severed the arm.

Outside the chamber, a great howl sounded, like that of a stormwind. Teirnyon, still carrying his sword, flung himself after it. In the darkness he could see nothing, but something dropped at his feet – a golden-haired infant, wrapped in a length of fine brocade. He picked the baby up. It was a boy.

Teirnyon gave the baby to his childless wife to rear, and the couple treated him as their own son. Only when the boy reached the age of four and rumors of the sad tale of Rhiannon reached him did Teirnyon recognize in the child the unmistakable features of the Prince of Dyfed. Kindly and honorable man that he was, he set out at once to restore Pwyll's child to him.

The meaning of these events was a mystery to the chroniclers. What creature had stolen Rhiannon's child and left him in faraway Gwent, they could not say. Nor could they tell why it attempted to steal a foal to accompany the child, although some thought this signified the boy's exalted blood: The people of that time worshipped horses as divine. But the kidnapper seemed to be one of the members of the Fair Family, who numbered dark and cruel beings among their kind. Perhaps to punish the mortals who had taken the Princess, this creature tried to recover the half-fairy child, showing the same hostility toward the alien race as Pwyll's people showed to Rhiannon.

At least, that would seem to be the case. It was as if the world of enchantment and the world of humankind – the one so fluid and complex, the other so prosaic – could not meet without misunderstanding and tragedy. Yet for all the sadness, there was a saving grace: Teirnyon's good action. It put an end to the worst of the pain and brought the blighted lives back into balance.

Ancient Metamorphoses

Nature was changeable when the world was young and magic still at play. Surrounded as they were by mysteries, humans saw evidence of transformation almost everywhere.

According to the Greeks, for instance, their sunflower — a kind of marigold — had not always been tied to the soil. The blossom began life as a water nymph named Clytie, who one day was cast out of the cool green depths of the sea and onto a sandy island shore. Entranced by the brightness, she rested there and followed with longing eyes the golden globe of the sun as it rode the heavens. Then a change came over her. Her mermaid's tail coiled down into the sand, rooting her in place; her silvery hair curled into petals around her face, and from her fingers, green leaves grew. By the ninth day of watching, she had become the sun's flower, whose blossom reflected the golden disk and followed its course throughout each day.

The Blood-Begotten Anemone

To the ancients, the crimson anemone was precious, for they believed that its petals were made from the blood of the god of growing things. It happened this way:

Aphrodite, goddess of love, conceived a passion for the god Adonis, he whose name meant simply "lord," whose beauty surpassed that of all creatures, and who ruled the things of the earth. For some months, the pair were lovers. Adonis, however, grew restless; despite the goddess's warnings, he went hunting in the wild one day and was gored by a boar.

The goddess found him as he lay dying, the bright blood from his wound spilled on the grass around. She wailed for him, and in her grief and love, she turned the scarlet splashes to the most delicate of flowers, called anemones, or "wind flowers," because the wind opened their petals and the wind blew them away all too soon.

There was more to the tale. It was said that Aphrodite begged the god Zeus to let Adonis return alive to her for part of each year. The plea was granted. Ever after, Greek women bewailed his autumnal death and rejoiced for him in the spring, when the blossoming of anemones signified his return to life and the renewal of the earth's fertility.

Tree-Guardians for a Temple

On a hill in Asia Minor once, near the ruined columns of a temple, there stood an oak and a linden, whose intertwined branches cast a kindly shade for shepherds of the region. In the noon heat, the men rested and told how the trees had come to be.

Long ago, the shepherds said, a village lay at the base of the hill. One day, a pair of wayfarers arrived, dusty, footsore and seeking shelter. They were turned brusquely away: The villagers had no use for strangers. The travelers trudged up the hill. Near the summit, in a reed-thatched cottage, they found a welcome at last.

The little house belonged to a man named Philemon and to Baucis, his wife, both bent and old. Theirs was a poor house, but they greeted the strangers with shy smiles, freely offering what they had – olives and soft cheese and cool wine in beechwood cups.

A curious thing happened during the meal. Though all drank deeply, the cups remained full, a sign that gods were in the house.

It was so. One of the strangers was Zeus, lord of the immortals; the other was Hermes, god of travelers and the road. The pair had a punishment for the villagers at the foot of the hill. They sent a flood to drown them. But they made the house of Philemon and Baucis into a temple, with the old people its priests. And the gods granted the couple's wish that neither should survive to grieve for the other. When Baucis and Philemon reached the end of their lives, leaves sprouted from their gnarled fingers, and their wrinkled flesh hardened to bark. They stood then as oak and linden, shading passing shepherds as graciously as they had served the gods.

Watcher of the Road

Along the country lanes of Europe grows the starry-flowered plantain, clinging to the verges of the paths as if seeking human company. The Germans of old times called the plantain *Wegewarte,* or "watcher of the road," and in that name lies the story of its genesis.

A maiden, people said, left her village one night and followed a path into a wood to meet her lover. He never came to her. Throughout the night, she waited for the sound of his footsteps, but all she heard was the hooting of the owls and the sigh of the wind in the trees, and in the small hours, she began to weep.

Finally, she lay by the path and died. The sun rose. All around her body, green shoots began to grow. By noon, pale blossoms had threaded their way through the dark strands of her hair. By evening, the body had vanished into a mass of tiny flowers. They haunt roadsides still, keeping vigil for a lover who never appears.

The Price of a Weaver's Pride

If Greek tales are true, the mother of spiders was Arachne, a Lydian maid so sure-handed and deft that no craftswoman could match her in spinning or in weaving. But Arachne was arrogant. Not even the gods could emulate her skill, she said – not even Athena, protector of all spinners and weavers.

It was true that Athena was patroness of these arts of peace, but she was also the goddess of war, and she lost no time in answering Arachne. She challenged the maiden to a contest of skill.

In her offering for the contest, Arachne added impudence to arrogance. She wove a scene that showed an awful creature – part man and part bull – taking a mortal woman. This, she said, represented the loves of the gods. Athena wove a scene of a mortal man strapped into a harness that supported wings made of feathers; the man had clearly flown too near the sun, for the feathers were already aflame. This, she said, was an image of human arrogance.

Then the goddess destroyed the mortal woman's work and, with a sharp command, the woman herself. At Athena's words, Arachne shrank and blackened, and eight wispy legs sprouted from her body. She spent the remainder of her brief life – as her descendants always would – spinning thread from her own belly and shuttling back and forth across its sticky strands to weave herself a web.

M.M.

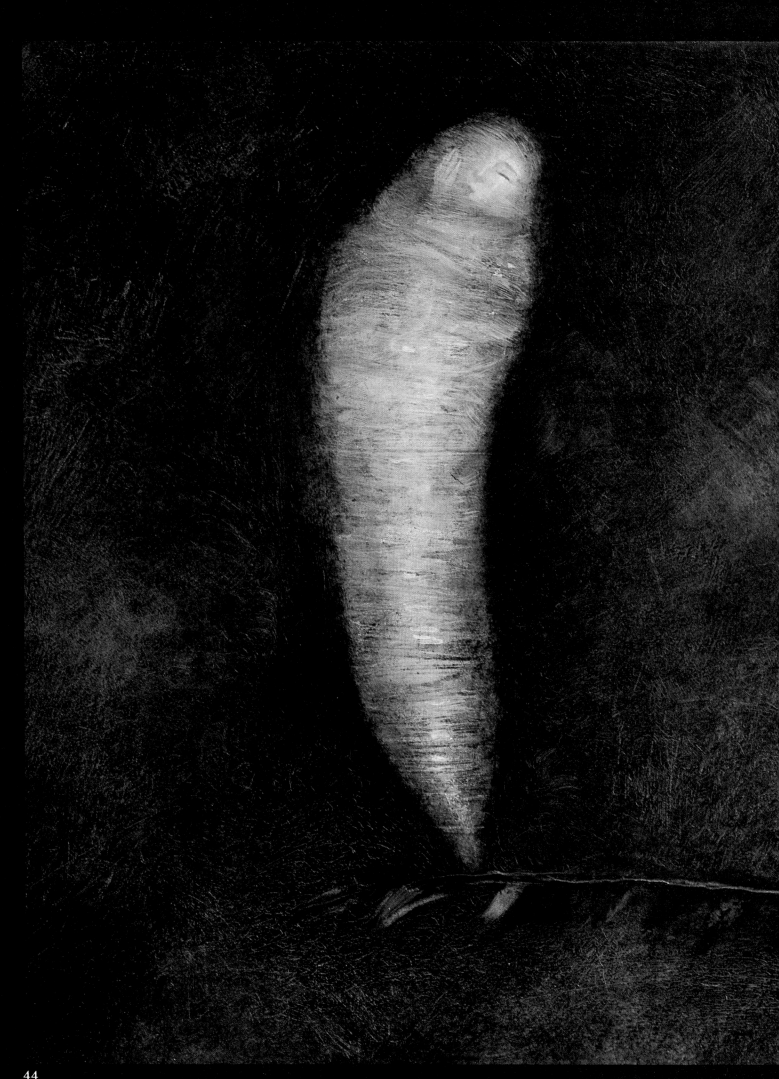

A Maiden's Silky Winding Sheet

Of the silk they prized so highly, the Chinese told this tale:

A warrior who lived in central China was sent to defend the country's borders; he left behind a wife and daughter. The maiden mourned excessively. She said aloud one evening that she would marry whoever brought her father home to her. After she had spoken, a stallion in her father's stables broke free and escaped into the night.

The horse reappeared some weeks later, bearing the maiden's father on its back. No one ever knew how the horse had found the man and induced him to ride home. But here the animal was, and as soon as the father dismounted, it became uncontrollable. Whinnying and puffing, the stallion pursued the daughter wherever she went, until at last she confessed to her father the vow she had made.

Horrified, the father killed the animal, flayed it, and hung the hide in the courtyard of his house to dry. But there was magic in that beast. When the daughter ventured into the courtyard, the hide freed itself from the wall, floated through the air as lightly as a fisherman's net, and wrapped itself around the maiden. Up into the air it flew with its prisoner, shrinking as it disappeared from view.

Some hours later, the father discovered on a mulberry tree all that was left of the horse and his daughter: a cocoon resting on a branch, enclosing a little worm. This creature spun from its body a fine, strong thread that, it was soon discovered, could be woven into fabric fit for a prince. And that, said the Chinese, was how the first silkworm came to be.

A Second Life for Love

In the days when galleys plied the Mediterranean, a curious calm sometimes came over the ocean around the period of the winter solstice: The gales ceased their howling, the sun broke through the clouds, and soon the waters lay still and glassy. These were the halcyon days, and during them, sailors said, the kingfisher made its nest on the deep. No storm would disturb the bird while it brooded over its young, the men claimed, for the kingfisher was protected by the gods. Here is the tale:

On the coast of Thessaly, there reigned a King named Ceyx, who took a bride called Halcyone. Though mortal, both had divine sires. Ceyx was the son of the morning star, and Halcyone was the daughter of the god of the winds.

Halcyone feared the power of the deities and wept when her husband left her to sail the seas. One night, a disturbing image of Ceyx came to her in a dream. He was pale and empty-eyed, with seaweed trailing from his beard.

In the morning, Halcyone left her palace to wander by the shore, and there she saw that the dream had been Ceyx's farewell, for his body floated on the waves. She flung herself into the waters then, but the gods took pity on her. Where the woman had been, a bright kingfisher took wing, and in a moment it was joined by another, for Ceyx was permitted to live again in this form with his wife.

And that is why, Greek sailors said, it was safe to voyage when kingfishers nested: On those clear days, no cloud would obscure the bright morning star, and no blast escape the guardian of the winds.

Starbound Beasts

Not all the natural wonders wrought through transformation are found on earth. A few are in the heavens – notably the Great Bear and her cub, which prowl the northern skies. Ancient stargazers were fond of telling how they came to haunt the night.

A young huntress named Callisto was loved by the god Zeus and bore him a son. The child grew to be a fine lad and a skilled hunter in his own right. But the union yielded grief in the end. Zeus's Queen, Hera, was enraged by the liaison and wove a spell of revenge: Where the lithe huntress had run, there lumbered a great bear, heavy of haunch, with matted fur and slavering jaws. In this form, Callisto found her son in the forest. She trotted toward him, and he, naturally enough, moved to slay the mighty creature with his spear.

But the pity of Zeus intervened. The god made his son into a second bear and flung the pair into the sky, to glitter forever as stars.

Chapter Two

Webs of Enchantment

Each autumn, when flocks of swans sailed in from the north on whistling wings and settled in cloud white drifts on the lakes of Ireland, the bards of that land were reminded of ancient mysteries. Sometimes they recounted stories of the gods of their ancestors, who traveled in the guise of swans. And sometimes they sang of cruel enchantments. Here is one such tale:

Long before the era when Christianity reached Ireland, before the time of mortal heroes such as Finn Mac Cumal, the country was ruled by a people who had magic to command. These were the Tuatha Dé Danann, a fairy race whose clans were united under the rule of a High King. At the time of this story, four clans answered to a leader called Bodb the Red. One of the clans was led by a chieftain named Lir, whose ties with the High King were close, for he married Bodb's foster daughter Aeb and took her to live in his fortress on the Hill of the White Field, near Armagh in what is now Ulster.

Aeb bore Lir two sets of twins—first a daughter, Fionguala, and a son, Hugh; then two sons, Fiachra and Conn. At the second lying-in, Aeb died, and Lir grieved deeply. He had loved his young wife, who had been a woman of singular sweetness and beauty, and now he possessed nothing of her but the four children.

So Lir mourned at length, until the High King, with rough kindness, sought to ease his pain. He sent Aeb's sister Aoife to be Lir's new wife.

It was a sensible arrangement and not an uncommon one at the time, for women frequently died young, leaving infant families behind. Aoife, who was called "the Fair and Wise," gained a powerful Prince for a husband; Lir gained a wife to warm his bed and serve as a mother to his children. Before many years had passed, however, new trouble began.

Its source was the children. Left to themselves in the first years after their mother's death, they had become close and secretive, the boys turning to the girl, Fionguala, for comfort and protection. So tightly knit were these four that they seemed to form a separate clan in the midst of Lir's busy court. Where they went, eyes followed them, for all had their mother's pale beauty and showed, as they grew, something of her charm. The children were scrupulously courteous to their stepmother, but as grave as old people. With their father, however, they romped like puppies, drawing him easily into their circle. When Lir heard their laughter in the mornings, he would leave Aoife's bed to watch them at their play.

Aoife, the childless stranger excluded from the family, began to watch Lir's children, too, first with bewilderment and then with coldness. Every averted glance, every polite evasion of her questions, every private smile at Lir she noticed and stored in her heart, until she sickened with envy. She gave no overt sign of anger, but when the time was right — when Hugh, the eldest boy, approached the age of seven and prepared to begin his warrior's training — Aoife set about accomplishing the removal of her rivals. She was adept in spells and enchantment.

A day came when the High King's messenger arrived at Lir's fortress bearing a summons for the children. Bodb the Red saw himself as their grandfather, and he wanted them trained at his own court.

"I will take the children south," said Aoife. This was not a surprising proposal. Many Irishwomen were excellent charioteers; some, in fact, fought beside their husbands in battle. Lir gave his assent with a smile: Aoife was a young woman and probably longed for an excursion herself.

But Fionguala put her hand in Lir's and said, "We will make the journey with our father, lady." Her brothers ranged themselves beside her.

Lir, however, did not tolerate defiance, even from his beloved sons and daughter. "You will ride south with your mother," he said. "I will follow later, when I can."

The children had to be content with this. So Fionguala and Hugh, Fiachra and Conn spent the next weeks traveling southwest across Ireland with their stepmother and a small train of her attendants. When Aoife guided the chariot, she was preoccupied with the horses and said little to the children; they stood behind her, ducking away from her snapping cloak. Sometimes, when she slowed to let the four of them walk along the rough track or when the company camped, the children found her observing them with dark, speculative eyes, but even then Aoife had few words for them.

They reached the shores of Lough Derravaragh, a shining sheet of water beneath the peak of the mountain called Knockeyon, and here Aoife called a halt to rest the horses. Although it was early in the day, she had the animals unharnessed and set to graze under the eyes of her servants. After the rest of the company had moved off, she summoned the children to the edge of the water.

"Into the lake, and wash off the journey's grime," said Aoife. The boys hesitated, but Fionguala indicated that they should obey, remembering her father's tone when they had balked earlier. She and the other children stripped and clambered shivering through the shore reeds and into the chill waters of the lake. Fionguala glanced back at her stepmother. She had knelt on the grass, apparently examining some small flowers that grew there.

A moment later, Fionguala looked again. Aoife was standing. Her arms were raised to the sky, and it seemed to answer the incomprehensible words she chanted.

The wind rose, and the clouds raced and boiled in the blue. Then she dropped her hands again. At once, the wind died and the waters ceased their dancing.

She turned to the lake. Where the children had splashed now floated four white swans. Their eyes were the dark blue of the children of Lir.

"An evil deed, stepmother," cried one bird in the light voice of Fionguala.

"I cannot undo it," said Aoife, and it seemed that her rage had been replaced by remorse. She stared at the swans for long moments. Tears coursed down her cheeks.

"What is the term of our captivity?"

Aoife's hands twisted slowly together as she told them the terrible terms of the spell she had made. "Ah, children," she said, "three hundred years here, on the waters of Derravaragh; and three hundred years in the north, on the sea between Erin and Scotland; and three hundred years in the western ocean by the island of Inishglora; and none shall release you until the woman of the south be mated with the man of the north. I cannot undo the spell, although I would now, if I could. But I can give you this. You will keep your human speech and memory, so that the enchantment will not wholly destroy you. And the music of your singing will be of a beauty never heard before on earth."

She strode away from the shore. The swan-children heard her giving orders: that the horses be harnessed, that the party move on. Then the bronze-bound chariot wheels clattered into the distance, and the shouts of the servants faded. And the swans were alone with the lisping of the water on the shore and soughing of the wind among the reeds.

Weeks went by. The four swans floated in the still waters, sometimes bending their long necks to see their white reflections and the moving images of clouds behind them. The great birds grieved and waited, for they were chained to this lake by Aoife's spell.

One day, the earth trembled with the drumming of hoofs, and a mounted company drew up to the shore. It was the children's father and his people, riding in search of them. Fionguala hailed him. Hearing his daughter's voice, Lir came to the water's edge where the swans were floating. He listened to the children's tale, and he wept to hear it.

Then, said the bards, Lir left the lake and pursued his wife to the court of the High King. He swept aside the lies the woman and her servants had told about the fate of the children. Bodb the Red punished her. He transformed Aoife into a demon of the air, to flap raven-like and alone forever in the night.

But even the High King could not break the terms of Aoife's spell. For three hundred years, the four swans glided on the waters of Lough Derravaragh and sang music so sweet that it eased the hearts of all who heard it. The swan-children never were alone in that time: Their father and his people and the people of all the clans of the Tuatha came to the lake to hear them. And during all that time, the storytellers say, Ireland was at peace.

But the second three hundred years of the enchantment were a different matter.

On an autumn day when the time had come, the swans rose from their lake and, with mighty wingbeats, headed north to the coast where basalt cliffs dropped into the icy, mist-shrouded sea the Irish called the Straits of Moyle. There, for three centuries, they braved the cold and the loneliness, singing high laments that could be heard sometimes by the folk on the Irish and Scottish shores.

When storms raged, they sheltered together on the rocks that fringed the cruel sea, and Fionguala was the shelterer, as she always had been in their childhood. She spread her wide wings over Conn on the right and Fiachra on the left, and she settled her brother Hugh under the feathers of her breast.

After that period of punishment was over, they flew west to the craggy rock of Inishglora, in the Bay of Erris. There they spent the final three hundred years.

At last, the term complete, the four swans rose as one and headed home to the Hill of the White Field, where Lir's fortress was. Over the land they sped, high above the clouds—across Connacht and Sligo and Leitrim and into Ulster. But when they descended, they found a wasteland. Everything had changed during their long captivity. In the words of the chronicler, the hill was "desolate and thorny before them, with nought but green

mounds where once were the palaces and homes of their kin, and forests of nettles growing over them and never a house nor a hearth." The Tuatha had vanished from the surface of the earth, retreating before the rising tide of humankind. These children were never to see their people again.

The tale says that the homeless, spellbound birds flew back to Inishglora, the last shelter they had known. There they met a member of the new race that had come to Ireland. A hermit saint named Mo Caemóc had settled on Inishglora in a round church he had built of stones. He kept the four swans under his care and made chains of silver to adorn their slender necks.

Their release indeed came when a man of the north married a woman of the south: A King of Connacht wed a daughter of the King of Munster. Having heard about the swans, relics of an earlier age, the King assaulted the saint's island chapel and tried to drag the birds off by their silver chains. But as he touched the chains, the metal fell away, and with it the feathers of the birds. The children of Lir stood revealed, no children now. In the swans' places, said the chronicler, were "three shrunken and feeble old men and one lean and withered old woman, fleshless and bloodless from extreme old age."

Their sad lives were at an end. And when the sister and her brothers died, the old monk buried them so that they sheltered together as they had during the winter nights at sea: Fion-

All spells had to play their patterns out: The children of the
Irish chieftain Lir, condemned to swan shape, regained humanity
only when the spell was done—and then they died of old age.

A brute born of clay

Many a tale of enchantment records how primal forces ran wild once they were unleashed. Jewish legends, for example, tell of spell-quickened creatures called golems that sometimes grew dangerously independent of their makers' wishes.

Golems were human figures molded from clay and brought to life by men schooled in sacred texts. It was said that rabbis animated the golems by placing in their mouths parchments inscribed with the name of God, at the same time reciting passages from the scriptures. Such rites were once performed as spiritual exercises – demonstrations of the power of the holy word.

But golems came to be employed for more mundane purposes. The most famous of these beings – the golem of Prague, named Joseph by the man who made him – defended the Jews in the Prague ghetto against the depredations of their Christian neighbors. Because the longer Joseph lived the larger and more powerful he grew, he was an effective deterrent to violence. He was also useful as a builder and errand boy: He could not speak, having no soul, but he could obey.

Like other creatures of magic, however, golems had a willful streak, and their ever-increasing size made them a threat to the very folk they were summoned to serve. So it was with Joseph, who ran amuck on a Sabbath eve for reasons no one could determine, leveling the ghetto walls with his massive shoulders and leaving buildings ablaze in his wake. He might have brought the entire ghetto to ruin had not his creator caught him, pulled the parchment from his lips, and recited backward the scripture that had started him into motion. All that was left when the man had finished was a lifeless mound of clay.

guala in the center of the grave, with Conn on her right, Fiachra on her left and Hugh lying across her breast.

The steadfast devotion of the children of Lir was remembered for centuries after stones covered their grave on Inishglora. Christians built a monastery on the rocky island, and people remarked that the air of the place had some quality of purification and preservation, as if the love of the four children lingered there still. The bodies of people who were buried on Inishglora did not decay.

The pain and waste of the lives of the children of Lir—centuries spent under the lash of wind and wave, imprisonment far from the father they loved—were punishments inflicted on innocents by a force that could not be contained or even moderated after it had been set loose. In her jealousy, the woman Aoife had made a spell of magic; when the spell was shaped into words, it formed a pattern of events that, no matter how much she regretted her action, could not be essentially altered until it had played itself out and the meanings of the words had been fully realized. A spell was a story (the word meant "tale"). Once it had begun, the story unfolded inexorably to the conclusion announced in the spell itself.

In those days, magic had power enough to alter the structure of existence and distort the very fabric of the universe. It thus held great dangers, especially in the earliest ages of the earth, when many beings had access to enchantment. And the risk extended to those who wielded the magic, as the tale of the children of Lir showed, for they could easily become victims of their own spells, as Aoife had.

In later eras, the masters of enchantment faded into invisibility. The humans who supplanted them as rulers of the earth remembered the earlier races in songs and stories, calling them fairies sometimes and sometimes old gods. But these predecessors were more than memories. For many centuries, the ancient ones continued to move among mortals from time to time, and men and women could catch glimpses of their primordial power.

The attitude of the oldest beings toward the human usurpers was equivocal at best—compounded, it seemed, of both love and hate. Considering the powers they still commanded, this attitude made them dangerous indeed. Tales that showed their omniscience and their hostility were part of even the oldest human myths of creation, where the first beings— soon to be supplanted—were the gods.

According to wise men of Greece, for instance, humankind was molded by the Titan Prometheus and given the breath of life by Zeus, lord of all gods. To lend power to the little beings he fashioned, Prometheus stole sacred fire for them. This he did against the will of Zeus, who feared that humankind would rise and destroy the gods if it was allowed to become strong. Zeus's punishment of the Titan came swiftly. He had Prometheus chained to a rock, there to hang for all eternity while an eagle tore at his flesh and devoured his liver.

The god also devised a spell-like punishment for humankind. He created a

Fearing humankind's increasing power, the Greek god Zeus gave the woman Pandora a casket sealed to mortal eyes. Curious, as the god knew she would be, Pandora raised the lid and so loosed a cloud of woe upon the world.

The evil of Morgan le Fay

One enchantress who wielded magic for contemptible ends was Morgan le Fay, a half sister of King Arthur of Britain. In her girlhood, wrote a chronicler, "Morgan le Fay was put to school in a nunnery, and there she learned so much that she was a great clerk of necromancy." She could appear as the most desirable of women or the ugliest of hags; she could fly; she could make illusions.

Mostly, Morgan le Fay used her arts as a means of pursuing her half brother and his Queen, Guinevere. She hated them, perhaps because in her youth they had separated her from her first lover, or perhaps simply because she was jealous of Arthur's greatness. In any case, she tormented the King, his wife and his warriors whenever she could. To seduce the men from the business of battle, she enchanted a valley; he who wandered into it was enspelled and condemned to spend his days idling hopelessly in a verdant paradise – a kind of death for a warrior. To destroy Guinevere, Morgan tried to reveal the Queen's infidelity with Sir Lancelot: She sent as a gift a magic drinking horn, which spilled its wine if the lady who drank from it was unfaithful. To attack the King, she wove spells into a glorious cloak and had a messenger carry it to Arthur; the garment would burn its wearer to ashes.

Yet repeatedly, she was defeated. The spell on the Valley of No Return, as it was called, could be lifted only by a man faithful to his lover; ironically, Lancelot – always faithful to the Queen – was the man who crossed its borders and thereby freed its prisoners. The drinking horn was not used in Arthur's court; it was sent on to the court of another King, Mark of Cornwall. And the cloak was thwarted by a warning from a fairy. Hearing of its danger, Arthur forced Morgan's messenger to wear the garment, and the woman died before his eyes.

As for Morgan, she faded into bitter retirement at last, far from the haunts of men.

woman. She was of astonishing beauty, and he saw to it that every skill was given her: She was charming, she was guileful, she was adept at the arts of love. This paragon he gave as a wife to a being named Epimetheus, who, although he was Prometheus' brother, lived in the world of men. She brought with her a dowry contained in a casket, which the god instructed was never to be opened, for the treasure in it was full of danger.

The husband hid the casket carefully, but the new wife was tormented by curiosity. At length she found the casket's hiding place. She took the box into her arms and hurried to a chamber where she would not be observed. Then she set the thing down and opened the lid.

It was a box of darkness. Shadows poured out of it and sailed up the walls of the room, out the windows, curling freely into the air. In their midst were horrors — the demons of poverty, of pestilence, of starvation, and of every vice that would haunt humankind in ages to come. As Zeus had foreseen, the woman was too frail to have charge of such an object as the casket. Her name, Pandora, meant, ironically enough, "all-giving."

Zeus's casket had the qualities of later enchantments. The little vessel was filled with forces that, having been released, could not be confined again. Its evils were tempered, in fact, only by something the casket itself contained: Storytellers said that Zeus had included among his cloud of evils one good — the gift of human hope.

The god's treatment of the newly formed and threatening race — his sending among them a woman bearing a burden of danger she did not comprehend — showed the same chuckling malice toward humankind that would be displayed by many later masters of enchantment. It was as if the elder peoples of the earth, still possessing powers that far surpassed human ken and knowing that mortals would rule the world when they themselves had disappeared, toyed with men and women's weaknesses for sport. To further their own ends, the creatures of the older world fashioned traps for the beings who would supplant them — spells and bindings set in motion by the actions of the mortals themselves. As if treating with foreign nations — which indeed humans were — enchanters offered spells as pacts, hedged about with limits and rules that were clearly delineated, if often baffling to human minds. It was the breaking of the rules that started the magic working in its preappointed pattern and brought about pain and sorrow.

The Irish, for instance, frequently recited the story of Gerald, Earl of Desmond, whose lands lay in County Kildare. His father was human, but his mother was a fairy named Áine. The Earl was famed as a warrior and a champion of the Irish — and he had an additional claim to renown. It was said that his ancestry gave him the power of changing his shape.

He married a human woman who longed to see the magic. He refused her, saying such things were best concealed from mortal eyes. But one morning, because the Earl loved his wife and because she begged so prettily, he yielded.

"I will change for your pleasure, lady,"

he said. "But the changing is a thing that frightens. You may not cry out when you see it; neither may you show any sign of fear, for if you do, the chains of the enchantment will bind me for generations under the earth."

The Countess replied proudly that she was the daughter of one great warrior and the wife of another. She had never shown fear, and she would not now.

"Watch, then," said the Earl, and he kissed her. He made no sign or sound, but in the next instant, the place where he had stood was vacant.

The Countess waited for some moments. Then a trilling sounded, and a small bird fluttered above her shoulders. She held out her hand, and the creature alighted there. It was a goldfinch. She smiled with delight, and the goldfinch cocked its shining head at her and winked roguishly (evidently the Earl was amused by his own power).

The bird gave a hop and landed on the window sill of the chamber. The Countess laughed to see it. Just at that moment, however, a fierce cry sounded outside the window. With a rush of wings, a hawk stooped toward the finch, talons at the ready. The Countess screamed and leaped to protect the little bird.

And that was the end. The goldfinch vanished, and the hawk, cheated of its prey, swerved and mounted into the sky again. The Countess was alone.

She remained alone for the rest of her life. Having inadvertently broken the laws of his enchantment, she never saw her husband again. Other people did, it seemed. The Irish said the Earl, with a band of warriors, slept for centuries in a cave under his own lands and that every seven years the company rode once around The Curragh—an enormous tract of pastureland in Kildare—mounted on white horses shod in silver. When the horseshoes had worn to the thinness of a cat's ear, said the storytellers, the Earl would return to life and reign as King of Ireland.

Most tales of mortals and magic in those early years displayed no such mutual sadness. Most stories were accounts of the last small triumphs of the old races over the new.

Sometimes the challenges of the masters of enchantment were so subtly declared that mortals simply ignored their gravity. Failing to recognize the dangerous nature of the beings they dealt with, men and women treated the magic lightly, and paid the price of carelessness.

Such was the case some years before the time of Gerald, when Finn Mac Cumal and his band of warriors patrolled the mountains and shores of Ireland. The warriors of the Fianna, as they were called, were a stellar company, trained and tested in every skill that men could have, from the chanting of Irish poetry to the wielding of weapons on the field of battle. Perhaps because they were the best of humankind, the men of the Fianna moved more easily than their humbler fellows between their own world and that of the elder races. In those days the people of the Tuatha—Lir's people—had long since vanished from ordinary human view. The portals to their invisible kingdoms had not

High was the price for flouting the terms of enchantment. Because his wife abused
his trust, Earl Desmond of Ireland vanished from her life to ride forever as a ghost.

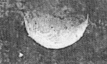

completely closed, however. Finn himself married a fairy and had a son with her, and many of his knights had ventured into the Tuatha's enchanted territories.

The very ease of movement seems to have engendered a certain arrogance in the Fianna. Among the warriors, for instance, was one named Iollan, a chief in his own right, who kept a fairy mistress. He treated her indifferently, a habit that would cost him dearly in the end. It was always a mistake to trifle with a fairy woman.

The beginning of their time together was idyllic. Few saw Iollan's lover, but of those who did, not one mentioned her name—which was Fair Breast—without speaking in the same breath of her lilylike beauty and her elusive, glancing charm. When Iollan wished for her, he simply spoke her name and she would docilely appear, moving just at the corner of his vision until he followed her into her own shifting world, which might be found at the turn of a path in a wood or at the edge of the sea or beneath the waters of a lake. For all the pleasures she gave him, Fair Breast asked only his fidelity in return. This he promised her.

"I hold you to your word," the fairy said. "If you fail me, Iollan, you must leave your people forever."

Iollan only laughed and drew her to him. There was no more talk that day.

But Iollan broke his promise readily when his leader Finn offered him a mortal bride. Her name was Tuiren; she was the chieftain's own kin and very precious to

him, so precious that Iollan had to pledge sureties for her safety. Then he took the woman to his own fortress and kept her there happily. He had not a thought for his mistress in the other world; he simply ceased to summon her.

Some months went by before Iollan saw his mistress again. When she appeared, he did not recognize her for Fair Breast. She rode into the courtyard of his fortress in the shape of a woman messenger of the Fianna, cloaked and booted and mounted on a sturdy pony. Her arrival caused a stir among Iollan's people, and he came out at once to greet her. After saluting her courteously, he asked her business.

"Finn sends greetings and requests that you attend him," said the messenger. The voice had an odd, lilting quality, faintly familiar, but Iollan did not notice this at the time. He was preoccupied with his new wife; already, he told his people proudly, Tuiren was with child. Besides, he had often seen the messenger's face among Finn's people.

"I will come," said Iollan.

"And I bear a message for your lady," said the woman. "From her kinsman."

"I will send her out to you."

Iollan sent a serving woman for his wife and headed for his stables.

The next part of the tale was told by Tuiren, Iollan's young wife. Finding Finn's messenger pacing beside her restless pony in the courtyard, she greeted the woman with gentle kindness. When the messenger asked if they could go to a place of privacy, Tuiren led her to her own sunny house, the pretty retiring chamber built for ladies in those days.

"Now tell me Finn's words," said Tuiren when the two women were alone.

But the messenger only stared at her for a moment, long enough to make Tuiren drop her eyes; she was a shy woman. Tuiren therefore did not see the cloak flung back and the rod of hazel wood that appeared in the messenger's hand. She heard the woman's voice sing a high, keening melody, but even that was lost in the next instant. The chamber walls reeled and leaped high around Tuiren; the very air whistled in her ears. Blackness descended on her, and when she came to her senses, she found herself gazing at the boots of Finn's messenger.

Tuiren cried out, and from her mouth came the anxious whimpering of a frightened dog. She backed away from the silent visitor and heard the scratching of a beast's nails on stone – nails that were her own. She had shed her woman's shape and taken that of a small hunting hound.

Above her head, the visitor said, "Try a few weeks as a hound, my lady. You will find it instructive. And stop that whining at once, or you will feel my whip."

She paused. "Here's a pretty mess," she added, and she began to laugh. The hound's swollen sides revealed what the woman's tunic had hidden.

Without further ado, the messenger scooped up the hound and made for her pony. Soon, she had left Iollan's fortress gate behind and was heading southwest across the countryside.

They rode for weeks, and during that ride Tuiren learned all varieties of humili-ation. She had to whine when she needed to be let down. She had to bark when she was offered meat, which she ate from the dirt, staring at the ants that crawled there. She found that she was a swift runner but, pregnant as she was, she could not keep pace with the pony for long. Her captor spoke little, except to give commands.

At last, they arrived at a gate. The messenger dismounted and set Tuiren down in the dust, remarking, "Here is a home for you for a while."

"Not here," a man's voice said. "No filthy hounds here; I won't have them about me." Tuiren cringed back against her captor's legs. A gentle boot in the side pushed her forward.

"This hound belongs to Finn, and he calls it his darling. He bids you care for it, Fergus. And do not hunt her now. She is near her time."

And so, grudgingly, Tuiren was taken into the hall of Finn's warrior Fergus, on the shores of Galway Bay, and cared for. When she first arrived, the man ignored her, but so dainty was she and so timid and humble, that at length she was allowed to lie by the hearth fire. Sometimes her new master even caressed her.

And what of Iollan? While Tuiren lived her dog's life in the stronghold of Fergus and Fair Breast drifted through her own shifting lands, peacefully awaiting events, Iollan searched.

He had to search. He had arrived at the fortress of the Fianna on the Hill of Allen, which rose among the water meadows of Leinster, only to find that he had not been summoned; he returned to his own stronghold, only to find that Tuiren had

Unwise was the man who betrayed the beings of Faerie. When an Irish warrior
    called Iollan abandoned his fairy mistress for a human wife, the fairy changed the
mortal woman into a hound and turned the animal over to a man who hated dogs.

disappeared. He questioned his people, but they could tell him nothing. He sent search parties through his territories and into the lands that marched with his, and still he found no sign of his wife. Months passed this way, and word of Tuiren's absence finally reached the ears of Finn.

Finn's response came quickly: Either Iollan would return Finn's kinswoman safe and sound to him, or Iollan would present himself for judgment and punishment. And the punishment for murder – which the disappearance seemed to indicate – would be severe. Iollan might be tied in a weighted sack and thrown into a pool to drown, or cast out to sea in a boat without sail or rudder, to drift until he died of thirst and exposure. And even should he escape death, he probably would be blinded – not an uncommon sentence then.

Iollan asked for more time to find his wife, and it was granted. He continued his frantic searching, but Tuiren was well hidden. Finally one day, driven perhaps by suspicion or perhaps by desperation, the hapless husband sat on a bench in his quiet hall, put his head in his hands and called the name of his fairy mistress.

With a faint rustle of silk, accompanied by a breeze that smelled of apple blossoms, Fair Breast appeared before him.

"Long months I have waited for your call," she said.

Her tone was sweet, with a curious lilt that brought to mind the courtyard and the woman messenger from Finn. Iollan raised his head.

"You have taken my wife," he said.

"She is quite safe, Iollan," the fairy woman replied, adding, "She has whelped two fine sons."

Iollan stared at her.

"She is a dog now, Iollan, a little greyhound bitch," said Fair Breast gently.

With a cry of fury, the Irishman sprang to his feet. Unmoved, his mistress told him that he himself had set her spells in motion when he broke his bond with her. Her terms now were simple: She could give Tuiren her true shape back and return her to Finn – thereby saving Iollan's life – only if he left his own world and came to hers to stay with her forever.

"And my sons?"

"Ah, Iollan," said the fairy, "I did not know she carried them when I wove the changing spell, and their names were not in it. They cannot leave the shape in which they were born." Fair Breast's face was expressionless as she spoke, but laughter bubbled in her voice.

That is how the warrior Iollan's name faded from the annals of the Fianna. As far as anyone knew, he disappeared into the Tuatha lands of Faerie to live under the rule of his mistress. Tuiren's true shape was restored to her, and Fergus took her home to her kinsman Finn, along with the two pups she had borne.

Eventually Finn arranged for Tuiren's marriage to a second husband, but he kept the two pups for himself, and in time they came to be his favorite hunting hounds. Their swiftness was famed, and their intelligence was almost human.

The account of Iollan's disappearance was not unusual in those days. Fairy people were desirable, and their gift of magic added to the temptation. Many men and women sought pleasures or power from them and, in consequence, died, or lost their true shapes and skulked through the world as animals or simply disappeared. Humanity, in the main, seemed never to learn that the folk and the things of the older world were full of jeopardy. Too often, mortals treated the elder races as lightly as Iollan had—and sometimes, human conduct was even worse than his.

Such was the case among the burghers of the Hanoverian town of Hameln many centuries ago. Hameln, settled since Saxon times, was a bustling place on the Weser River, prosperous from fisheries and from the grainfields that spread to the base of Mount Poppen, which loomed like a sentinel over the town. The people had city walls to protect them from enemies, a fine church to worship in and a cobbled square with a carved fountain, where the women gossiped in the mornings as they washed their linens and fetched water for their households.

Hameln also had the common pest of the medieval city, *Rattus rattus*—the black rat. These plague bearers, called "the devil's lap dogs," lived on the grain, the fish and the meat of the people; to prevent their powerful teeth from growing through their flesh, they wore the teeth down by gnawing on the walls of the people's houses. They nested comfortably under eaves and in walls and cellars, producing abundant young at frequent intervals. So numerous were they that cats could not control them. The rats quickly grew impervious to what few poisons were to be had and, being intelligent creatures, learned to avoid traps. They were impossible to eradicate, and the townsfolk simply lived with them, muttering impotently when food was stolen and children were bitten.

All of this changed in Hameln on a day in June seven hundred years past. A stranger wandered into the town, a tall and merry fellow dressed in the many-colored motley of a fool or a traveling jongleur. A little crowd gathered around him in the square, full of curiosity and chatter: Strangers were a very rare sight in those days. The newcomer asked for water, and this was given. He asked for bread, and this was given, too.

Then a guildsman of the town broke up the crowd and sent them about their business. "We don't care much for strangers here," he said. "How will you pay for the provisions we have given?"

The stranger only smiled and drew from his traveling sack a shawm, a reed instrument that was the ancestor of the oboe. "I will pay you with a song, father," he said. Raising the slender instrument to his lips, he blew a melody so clear and gracefully shaped that all who were within hearing paused in their work and listened and smiled. Not a word was spoken while he played.

When it was finished, the guildsman said gruffly—for he, too, had been caught in the spell—"What else can you do?"

"This pipe has many tunes," said the piper. "It does what I ask it."

Out of the town of Hameln scuttled all its rats, lured to their doom by the music of a magic pipe. When the burghers of the town would not pay the piper the price they had promised for his work, he fashioned another deadly tune.

This was magic. The guildsman called other townsfolk to him, and they consulted beside the fountain. Meanwhile, the piper moved a little way off, examining the narrow lanes that wound away from the square. Finally tiring of the whispering of his hosts, he said, "I can rid this place of rats with my pipe, if you like. For a price."

"What is the price?" said the guildsman.

"Thirty guilders would be right. I often have use for mortal gold."

So the bargain was struck. The townsfolk backed off and looked at the piper with expectation, but he merely smiled again. "Remember that you have entered a contract with me. You have agreed to the rules that I set. And remember that my pipe plays many tunes," he said. Then the piper crossed the square and passed through the town gate.

He reappeared the following morning, and the music of his playing pulled the townsfolk from their beds. Shutters were flung open, and heads appeared to watch the piper wind his way through the streets, dancing an odd little skipping dance to the tune he played on his pipe. Through every street he skipped, and where he went, rats followed. They poured out of windows and from cracks in foundations and from nests in the trees.

Soon a flood of furry bodies was rolling and humping along in the piper's path. So numerous were they that the scuttling pink paws made a sibilant sound on the stones of the streets.

When all the rats of the town had been gathered, he led them to the edge of the Weser River and waded in, piping all the while. The rats followed. By the thousands they poured over the banks of the river and paddled after the piper as he moved into deeper water.

Hours of pandemonium followed. Held by the music, the rats were not able to swim back to shore. They scrabbled helplessly, fighting the current and one another. The people of Hameln came to the river's edge and jeered and threw stones at the dying animals.

When nothing showed on the water but inert bodies, swirled by the current, the piper lowered his instrument. He waded out of the water. His clothes were dry.

He said to the guildsman, "It is finished, master. Now if you will pay me, I will be on my way again."

But the guildsman began to wheedle and haggle. Thirty guilders was too much, he said; he offered ten.

The piper heard him out and said, "Do not break your contract, mortal. Remember that you agreed to my rules. I told you my pipe played many tunes."

The guildsman shook his head and watched impassively as the other shrugged and turned away. The piper strode briskly along the path that led out of the city into the fields around. Presently his scarlet cap disappeared among the stands of grain.

He returned at dawn of the following day, and the music of his pipe preceded him, floating over the fields and through the town gate, across the square and into the narrow streets and the jumbled wooden houses. Wherever the music sounded, the grown people froze like statues in their beds or at their hearth fires.

But not the children. Out of cots, up from pallets, out of chairs the young ones surged, following the music into the street. They came in all the ages that could walk, from toddlers only a year old to boys whose voices had just begun to crack. Blindly and silently they followed the song, crowding the streets in their nightshirts and gowns. The piper's song laughed in the air, and behind him the children began to run and trip across the town and out the massive gate. That was the last that was seen of the piper and of almost all of the children. Of the town's youngsters, 130 disappeared.

Some days later, two children were discovered outside the gates of the town, bloodied and almost mute. One of them had been blinded; the other, it seemed, had lost his senses. The blind child said the stranger had led them through the fields and up the road that crossed Mount Poppen. A gate had opened in the mountain, and the child's fellows had followed the piper into it. But he had been too slow; the wall of bramble-covered hill had closed upon him, and after that, he remembered no more.

When he awoke sometime later he lay on the road, with the other child whimpering beside him. He felt along the side of the mountain where the opening had been, but no gate was there; none was ever to be found.

The people of Hameln never forgot the calamity. For centuries, they dated town events from the day their children left them. When a new town gate was built, they inscribed these words on the stone: *Centum ter denos cum magus ab urbe puellos*

duxerat ante annos CCLXXII condita porta fuit, which meant, "This gate was built 272 years after the sorcerer abducted 130 children from the city."

As if compelled, they passed their tale down through the generations, reminding children and grandchildren and all who came after of the folly of their ancestors and of the sorrow it had brought upon the town. Those who dared to treat with the beings of the old world, they said, must follow the rules those beings set forth. Safety lay only in following the patterns of enchantment precisely as those patterns were revealed.

And to make sure the children did not forget, the people of Hameln fashioned a grim reminder of the piper and his power: The cookies of that town were baked in the shape of rats.

An Embowered Sleep

The magic that once sang freely through the world was a force that few mortals could comprehend or resist. Words alone, if spoken by those with power, could engender a pattern of events that were bound to continue until that pattern was complete. A French tale describes the inexorable workings of one spell:

A lord and his lady lived once among the verdant hills of Burgundy. They were cousins, scions of a venerable house, and their life was pleasant in almost every way, for their lands were rich. Vineyard, field and pasture gave forth abundance; it was said that the very roses in the gardens of their palace bloomed in a profusion that nothing could restrain.

In only one respect did the realm's fecundity fail: The couple was childless. Early in the marriage, this seemed no great thing, but as the years passed, the people of their little court began to whisper in the corridors and to question chambermaids and laundresses. If the lord and lady heard the talk, they gave no sign; his demeanor, perhaps, became more arrogant, but she continued as she always had been, blithe and gay. And the day came, in the middle of their lives, when they told their people that the lady was with child.

The infant was born in due course – a daughter destined to be a great heiress – and the celebrations were splendid. In the fields and villages, the common folk built bonfires, so that at night the countryside twinkled. In the palace there was feasting, and the halls blazed with candlelight and rang with music.

On the child's naming day, however, a shadow of evil spread through the

court. It happened that, among his company, the lord had a number of wise women who, while they appeared to be court ladies like any others, were credited with mysterious power. Some said that these women had fairy blood, and this may have been true, for fairies mixed more freely with mortals then.

In any case, all of these women gathered at the naming feast, as was their right. One of them, for reasons no one could ever afterward explain, cursed the infant. Towering menacingly over the cradle, the woman hissed, "This girl child shall die just before she becomes a woman. She will prick her finger on a spindle, and the wound will kill her."

The musicians fell silent, and a tremor ran through the company. The child's nurse crouched fiercely over the cradle and thrust the speaker back. But in the hush, another voice said softly, "I cannot undo this action, Sister, but I can alter its shape. The child will not die. She will sleep for a hundred years, and the day she wakes, she will become a woman." The two wise women stared at each other for a moment; then in the place where they had stood, there was only empty air.

As for the lord and lady, they did what they could to protect the child. They forbade the presence of either distaff or spindle in the palace, and they did not allow their daughter to leave the grounds. She passed her girlhood in this pretty prison and never saw the spinning of flax or wool.

Every great old house has forgotten rooms, however. When the girl was about fifteen and given to wandering restlessly through the halls, she came upon a dusty tower chamber. It was empty of furnishings, but an old woman sat in a recess in the wall. The woman raised an arm to hold a flax-laden distaff; her other arm descended as she pulled threads and twirled them onto a spindle.

The maiden was delighted at the sight. She went forward curiously. Without a word, the crone rose from her place and passed the distaff and spindle to the maiden. And the maiden's finger slipped across the point of the spindle. She staggered a moment, then she slid soundlessly to the floor. The old woman chuckled softly and disappeared.

The maiden was found some hours later, rosy as she always was, but still as in death. Her breath barely misted a mirror held before her lips. She was carried

to her own chamber. Her grieving parents laid her on her bed in state, and they stayed at her side, weeping.

But a curious thing happened in the palace that day. Some said it was the work of the wise woman who had tempered the curse. In order that the maiden should not wake among the dead – for those around her would not survive a hundred years – this woman drifted through the palace corridors whispering, and where she walked, she cast a spell of sleep. In the great kitchens, the cats lay motionless on the window sills, the cooks nodded at their long tables, the fires dwindled and died, and the little dogs that turned the cooking spits collapsed on their treadmills. In the palace halls, the courtiers slid to the floors. In their daughter's chamber, the lord and lady leaned against each other and slept. And all around the palace walls, green

shoots trembled and reached toward the sky. Up along the stones they crept, mere tendrils at first, but filled with restless energy. Before long, they reached the top of the walls, and then the tendrils began to swell and thicken and send out blossoms, forming a mass of thorns and roses to curtain the castle. Within hours, the enchantment was complete, and nothing could be seen of the palace but the faintest glimmer of the towers when the sun struck their gilded turrets.

For a hundred years, the great rose mound stood unchanged. After a time, the region lapsed into wilderness. The villagers left that haunted country, taking their children, cattle and whatever they could load in carts. Grapes withered on the vine, and grain dried in the fields. Houses and barns crumbled. Blight settled on the trees, and soon the land was sere and brown, deserted except for occasional lonely shepherds and their flocks, who quickly left.

From time to time throughout the century, an adventurer would cross that barren waste and glimpse the towers within the hedge. Then he would try his strength against the wall of briars, hacking at it with sword or ax. But the roses were strong with spells and always held against the intruder. They did more than hold. With thorny fingers that clutched and curled, they wound around his neck and plucked at his arms, coiling and darting like serpents. Once he was firmly gripped, they pulled him into the heart of the living wall, and there the adventurer would die. Soon his flesh would dissolve, and only the bones were left to hang in the trap, a mute warning to any who would dare the barrier. In their pride, many dared, and all perished.

Then one came who was different. On a day early in May, a young man — a part, no doubt, of the spell itself — rode boldly across the desolate fields.

He dismounted at the wall of thorns and examined it closely. With his sword, he touched a branch. At once, the roses brightened. The briars opened their arms and made a path for him.

He walked through shadowed courtyards and darkened halls, stepping over the bodies of the sleepers, until at length he found the chamber of the maiden. Striding to the bed where she lay, he bent and kissed her. She opened her eyes and smiled at the stranger who soon would be her husband.

As she smiled, bells rang in the corridors. The lord and lady woke; the courtiers in the halls stirred and rubbed their eyes. In the kitchens, the fires leaped to life. Dogs barked, and cats yawned and stretched. A century after the words of magic had been spoken—a hundred years to the instant—the pattern of enchantment had completed its ordained course.

Chapter Three

Deliverance from Magic's Coils

In times gone by, the people of Wales told stories of the Well at the World's End, a spring whose waters gave life, although not always in the ways the seeker might expect. The well itself was elusive. Like many other things of Faerie, it might appear to the unsuspecting traveler in any secret place—in a cave in the severe heights of Snowdonia, for instance, or in a hidden thicket in the forest of Radnor. Some said the well could be found along the cliffs of the coasts. And generations of a certain great family told that the well had been discovered once by an ancestress of their own, in the green and peaceful Tywi Valley in the south.

That discoverer was the daughter of the lord of the region, powerful enough to be called Prince. An only child, she was merry and willful, and at the time of her adventure, she had escaped her various attendants and gone alone into the countryside that spread around her father's hall. She idled along the bank of a narrow river that lay in coils across the land, dividing the golden grainfields. Without hurry, easily avoiding the men at work in the fields, she made for the woods upstream. The voices of the men and the rhythmic hissing of their scythes

faded away, and she entered the forest shadows. Here, the river was a bubbling stream that made a stone-studded pathway through the trees.

She followed it to a place where the water rose from the forest floor. At this spot, the Princess paused. The wood had become extraordinarily shadowy; trees gathered around her, trailing branches toward the water. The only sounds to be heard were the rustling of leaves and the whispering of the water among its stones. The very air seemed still and listening.

The Princess sank to her knees beside the spring. From a chain at her waist she detached a hollow golden sphere—a pierced pomander ball, made for holding sweet-scented herbs. She turned the pretty thing in her hands a moment; then she held it over the spring to observe the watery reflections on its gleaming surface.

But her hand was wet, and the sphere slipped from her fingers. For an instant it floated, flashing gold; then, with a gurgle, it sank. Swiftly the maiden reached, but not swiftly enough. Her hand closed on emptiness in the pool's icy depths.

She leaned over the spring, staring into the water and biting her lips. The pomander was a woman's jewel, not a girl's. The gift of it to her was a sign that she had left her childhood behind. Now no glimmer of gold shone in the dark pool – only her own face, shadowy in the water.

The surface of the pool shivered, fragmenting the reflection. Somewhere quite near, a voice – a small, throaty, gulping voice – spoke. "Would you have your jewel back, lady?" it said.

The Princess sat back on her heels and peered around, but no one was there. The trees waited silently. On its edging stones, the water rippled.

"Speak again," said the Princess.

A head broke the water's surface. With a powerful kick, a frog sprang up and landed on the stones around the spring. Dripping, it surveyed her. Its mud-colored eyes bulged from an aged, mottled face ludicrously fixed in a frog's wide, lipless grin. The Princess drew her skirts back out of harm's way, but she held her ground.

With a heave of its swollen sides, the small beast spoke again. "You will forgive my discourtesy, lady," it said. "I am not made in a shape for bowing."

"What are you?" asked the Princess.

"A frog, as you see. I am the guardian of the World's End Well, which holds your golden ball."

"Can you fetch the ball for me?"

"I can return the ball to you, yes. I am no servant to fetch. But there is a price."

"And what is the price?" asked the Princess. She had heard that enchantments could make beasts speak. Still, it was hard for her to keep from laughing at this ugly little creature.

"Why, the price is that you make a pet of me and feed me from your own dish

and take me into your own bed to be beside you. And one more thing, which I cannot yet name." The bulbous eyes blinked shut and slowly open.

"Indeed, I will pay, frog, if you will but give me my ball," said the Princess.

Without another word, the frog flopped into its pool and vanished, trailing bubbles. When it resurfaced, its mouth was stretched around the glistening metal of the pomander.

The Princess took the ornament from the frog's jaws. As she did so, her fingers brushed its slick and chilly head. She shuddered and rose to her feet.

"My thanks, beast," she said, but her face was set into lines of revulsion. With a whisk of skirts, she turned and made quickly down the stream for home.

Behind her, the frog leaped from its pool. Sometimes hopping across rocks and through reeds, sometimes crawling awkwardly, always keeping close to the water, it set out along the lengthy path the Princess had taken.

As for the Princess, she crossed the fields quickly and slipped into the courtyard of her father's fortress. It was a jumble of wagons and shouting men; the people were bringing in the harvest, and the Princess's absence had gone unnoticed.

That night, however, when the maiden sat with her father in the high, private chamber built above his hall, her adventure was revealed. In the hall, the long tables were laden, and her father's people – soldiers and servants alike – were noisily celebrating the gathering in of the crops, but this little chamber was quiet. Its tapestries muffled the sounds from below, and father and daughter ate in peace.

Midway through the meal, a small, deep voice sounded from near the Prince's boot. "Lord, grant me a hearing," it said.

The Prince looked about until he spotted the frog, crouching among the floor rushes. He was a wise man, used to the beings that hid in Wales. He said, "I hear."

"Water, lord," said the frog. The Prince picked the creature up gently and slid it into the silver basin kept for the washing of hands after meals. With a sigh, the frog slid into the water. Caked bits of mud and straw floated off its dry back, and it closed its eyes. At length, it spoke again and told how the Princess had found it, how it had served her and what she had promised.

When it had finished, the Prince said, with more sternness than she had ever known from him, "Is this true, daughter? You gave your word?"

The Princess shrugged impatiently. "I said that I would pay. But this is a beast, lower than a slave."

"Nevertheless, pay you must." And under her father's relentless eye, the Princess had to tear scraps of bread and feed them to the frog. She did it sullenly, turning her head away when the beast's long tongue flicked out to seize the food.

When the meal was finished, she obeyed a signal from the Prince and took the frog up the stair that led from his chamber to the tower room where she slept. She carried the beast by holding a cold hind leg between her thumb and forefinger, although the frog panted miserably and pawed at her wrist with rubbery toes.

Tossing it onto the end of her bed, she climbed in and pulled the covers close. In the small hours, however, the frog dragged itself over the bedclothes and settled down next to her. She lay awake for a time, rigid with distaste, feeling its heartbeat fluttering its damp, distended sides.

In the morning, the frog was there still. It had moved to the blanket that lay across her shoulders, and it crouched motionless, staring at her with its old man's eyes and grinning its fixed grin.

"Princess," it grunted when it saw she was awake. "You have fed me by your hand and warmed me by your flesh. Now there is but one act left. When it is done, the terms I gave will be fulfilled."

"What is it?" asked the maiden.

"Cut off my head and free me from this life."

She flinched at that, but she arose. Shivering in the morning chill, she waited while the frog crawled to the edge of the bed and fell heavily to the floor, where it lay stretched out and submissive. It said nothing more. When she stabbed into the neck with the dagger that lay beside her bed, its legs twitched convulsively, but that was all. For long, miserable moments after that, the Princess sawed at the frog's thick neck, until at last the head was free. Strangely, no blood flowed from the wound. As the last tendon parted, the skin of the frog fell open on the floor. It was empty. W i t h i n seconds, it had shriveled, crackling drily, and crumbled to a powder.

A low laugh brought her head around. By the window, entirely at his ease, stood a tall young man, dressed in the velvet surcoat and furred cloak of a lord; a circlet of gold crowned his dark hair. He was smiling at her.

"My thanks, lady," he said. "That life was a dull and lonely one." Then he threw his cloak around her shoulders and, taking her hand, led her down the stairs to her father's chamber.

So, according to her descendants, the Welsh Princess fulfilled the terms of a spell and relieved a lord of an enchantment that had bound him in beast's shape and set him as guardian to the Well at the World's End. The family's story was vague about the source of the spell, but the resolution was clear enough: The lord took the maiden for his wife.

In the era when the Princess lived, magic was still a familiar force in the world. Many beings who controlled it lingered on, hidden away from human sight. Invisibility was their last retreat. They were ever watchful and, it seemed, ever hostile to the men and women who ruled lands where they themselves once had freely walked.

The nature of their magic had not changed. As before, it was charged with both delight and danger; its spells still formed patternings that had to be worked through before the grip of the magic was released. But now more than ever, spells served as tests of the character of humanity. They were the final challenges issued by the old world to the new—the last battleground, in effect.

It might be that enchantments tested honor, as the frog-lord tested the Princess. The terms of some spells were challenges to wit or courtesy or simple human kindness. And some magic, by placing mortals in terrible jeopardy, tested the most basic of human virtues in that perilous age: courage and loyalty.

Accounts of such threatening enchantments for the most part were monuments to the valor of kings and their warriors. The chronicles of Arthur of Britain reverberate with such reports: His knights wandered the world in search of adventures that would test their mettle. Arthur's knight Gawain, for example, once came upon a fortress called the Castle of Wonders, which had long served as a prison for undefended mortals—fatherless maidens and landless widows. Only a matchless knight, it was said, could release these people. The castle was defended by five hundred longbows that fired of their own accord at any man who attacked it and by a giant lion that tore apart any who survived the arrows. Gawain, however, braved the arrows and beheaded the lion, ending the mortals' captivity.

Much later, Gawain's son, Gingalin, was sent to rescue a Welsh Queen bound in dragon form by sorcerers. Her prison was a city called Senaudon, which itself was enspelled and had become a barren wasteland. Gingalin found the place. He rode alone through its crumbling gate and deserted streets. When he entered the hall of the city's palace, axes flung by invisible

Reluctantly bound by her word, a Princess took a frog for a bedfellow. In doing so,
she fulfilled the terms of an enchantment and released the creature into its human form.

hands attacked him, and a knight mounted on a fire-breathing horse assailed him. Gingalin stood his ground against the flight of axes and was unharmed. Next, he slew the knight. Then he found the dragon, gave the beast the kiss that released it, and thereby lifted the enchantment on Queen and city.

Such were the tales the valiant told. Many stories, however, record the quieter deeds of plainer folk, who did not seek out the magic of the elder age but found themselves its victims. Among these accounts lies a story whose human champions were not knights but a merchant's daughter and her brothers.

The tale began in Paris, in the age when the Île Saint-Louis was still partly a pasture used for the city's cows and the bridges that arched the Seine were lined with the houses of the city's goldsmiths and moneylenders, its vintners and merchants.

On one such bridge, the Pont Notre Dame, in a comfortable, half-timbered house whose walls shimmered with reflections from the water that flowed below, lived a prosperous *marchand de l'eau* – a water merchant who owned barges that plied the Seine carrying grain, salt and wine. With him were his two sons and a daughter, whose name was Isabelle. This young woman was beautiful in the fashion much admired at the time – as small and slender as a child, with a child's pearly skin and high, rounded forehead. In the trailing gowns and many-folded linen headdresses that women wore then, she gave the appearance of flower-like vulnerability; in

fact, Isabelle, whose mother was dead, had been in charge of her father's house and servants since her childhood. She was quite accustomed to command.

It was not surprising that the water merchant's daughter attracted the attention of her father's fellows; it was more surprising, however, that she aroused the interest of a lord, for the dukes and counts whose graceful city palaces lined the riverbank looked higher than the bourgeoisie for their wives. But that is what happened, and Isabelle was summoned late one October afternoon to her father's chamber to be presented to a noble suitor.

She paused at the doorway to observe the man while he talked with her father and brothers. So large and powerful was he that the others seemed shrunken; indeed, the very paneling of the room seemed smaller. He was dark-haired, very white of face; his eyes were heavy-lidded; and from his nostrils, two deep grooves ran down to disappear into a beard so black that blue lights glinted in it. His mouth showed in the beard, and the thin lips were of a scarlet color unusual in a male. Although he wore the black robe of a widower, he did not seem bereaved: The robe was of a stiff brocade edged with miniver, and jewels glittered on his hands.

All this Isabelle saw in the brief moment before her father turned and, with a genial sweep of his arm, beckoned her into the room. "Ah, Count," he said, "my girl, as you see. Now, then, Isabelle."

With composure, Isabelle entered the room and made her curtsy to the black-haired Count. He drew her closer to him and gazed down at her. With a cold, white finger he traced the line of her cheek and throat and breast. "A tender city maid," he said softly. Her brothers, who had maintained a grim silence throughout the scene, stirred angrily at the gesture, but the Count ignored them. His hand dropped to the keys Isabelle wore on a ring at her waist, signifying her position as mistress of her father's house. "I shall give you keys to better rooms than these."

Then, apparently losing interest in her, he turned to her father and said, "I will send my steward to you about the matter of the settlements." And he strode out, attended by the bowing merchant, whose chattering he appeared not to notice.

As soon as the Count had left, Isabelle's brothers closed around her, speaking furiously of insults and arrogance. But Isabelle did not reply. Her eyes were fixed on the archway where the Count had gone, and they were bright with desire. Her cheeks were rosily flushed.

"That man is old, he is debauched, he has buried two wives that we know of. You will not have him, Sister," said the older of her brothers.

"I will," said Isabelle.

Within a month she was a wife. And a week later, traveling in a horse-drawn litter with her husband on horseback beside it and a train of storage carts and pack mules following, she left Paris for the Count's lands in Brittany. Her brothers bade the couple farewell civilly, but the younger one, sensing some change in Isabelle that perplexed and disturbed him, grasped her hands at the last and said, "If you should summon us, we would come to you, Sister." The Count leaned from the saddle and twitched the litter's curtains shut.

When they had left Paris behind, however, the Count remarked, "Your brothers seem to think I hurt you, young wife." The only answer that came from the litter was a sleepy chuckle.

The house where the Count took his bride was a castle, forbiddingly walled and bristling with polygonal, slate-roofed towers that seemed to float on the black waters of a lake. The forest that pushed toward it along the lake shore was bare now, and the only sounds were the harsh winter crying of the rooks in the trees.

A forbidding picture, perhaps, but Isabelle hardly saw it, nor did she notice the icy December rains that hissed on the roof tiles and pocked the waters of the lake. For the most part during her first months there, she kept to the round chamber the Count had given her, where the air was warm and scented from the applewood logs that burned continuously on the hearth; where flowering tapestries moved gently on the walls; where the bed was high and soft and hung with silk. Her husband would stay by Isabelle's side for long hours; then he would disappear from the chamber, busy perhaps on his own affairs, and as abruptly reappear, bearing jewels to adorn her and wine to keep her warm.

Lost in pleasure, Isabelle drifted and dreamed, but at last she grew restless. Late one morning, as he arose from her bed, she said to her husband, "You keep me a prisoner of delight, my lord."

He laughed and flicked her throat gent-

A fiendish being who married mortal women only to murder them, Bluebeard possessed
a golden key that signaled the moment for killing: It began to bleed uncontrollably.

ly with his white fingers, but he said only, "More delights will come to you, Isabelle." He left her.

When he returned, however, Isabelle was up, clothed in gown and overdress, her hair hidden modestly in a wimple of linen. The Count raised his black brows. Then he smiled and said, "So eager to assume the burdens of a wife?" Onto the bed he threw a ring of keys and added, "Here is the banner of the chatelaine, then."

He gave a call for his steward, a sly, secret man with a knowing smile. Then he crossed his arms, leaned against the bedpost and listened while the steward told her the uses for the keys: this for the buttery, where the wine was kept, this for the grain stores, this for the silver cellar, this for the jewel casket.

"And the golden key?" said Isabelle, when all but one had been named. The steward shrugged.

"That key unlocks my own chamber," said her husband. "You are never to enter it. It is private to me."

"Very well," said the wife, and lowered her eyes demurely.

From that time, Isabelle assumed the proper wife's role, for which she had been so well prepared in her father's house. In a few weeks, when she had learned the twistings and turnings of the old castle, and the steward, by her order, reported to her daily, the Count formally placed her in charge. He was needed in Paris, he said, and rode away through the the castle gate into the countryside just touched with the first faint green of spring.

Left to her own devices, Isabelle wandered. Though they were rarely visible, the Count's people were admirably trained, and she was carefully served; once she had given her orders to the steward each day, she had little to do.

So she paced the long gallery and examined the tapestries that hung there, shifting in the draft so the figures seemed to move. These hangings displayed hunting scenes, but none such as Isabelle had ever known. All the hunters were dark, bearded men like her husband; some were not fully men but manlike creatures with the horns and hoofs of goats. The women who rode there rode nude and white across the embroidered green fields, and the fields themselves were splashed with blood. Everywhere rabbits leaped into the air, transfixed by arrows; deer fell to their knees, spurting scarlet; birds fluttered helplessly in crimson pools. After a while, Isabelle tried another room and found the same scenes painted on the ceiling vaults: A race of dark men closing in at the kill floated above her head.

Her lips tight with distaste, she abandoned exploring and inspected the storerooms and the other chambers for which she had the keys. And when all the keys had been used but the one of gold, Isabelle did not hesitate. She was, after all, mistress of the house. She retraced her path through the tapestry gallery to a door that stood in a recess at one end. She turned the key in the lock and pulled the door of her husband's chamber open.

The chamber was a windowless room, thick with shadow, but even in the dim light its terrible inhabitants could be seen.

Isabelle, little knowing that she was the bride of death, used beard's key to open his secret chamber. She discovered the lifeless figures of nging there and thus learned what her own fate would be.

Betrayed by the bleeding of the key, Isabelle awaited the end that Bluebeard's magic demanded. But love fought the powers of the dark: Her brothers rode to rescue her.

They hung from ropes along the wall, heads lolling crazily, throats pierced by great meathooks. Some still had eyes, and these were open and staring blindly at her. Some were no more than skeletons. All were women as small as she, and all were robed in the white finery of brides. Beneath the bare and dangling feet of each were islands of dried and clotted blood.

Isabelle dropped the ring of keys to the bloody floor. With swift, shaking hands, she picked them up again, then backed out of that slaughterhouse and closed and locked the door.

The husband whose caresses had entranced her was a murderer, and she was imprisoned alone on his lands among his people. If she fled, he would find her, perhaps before she reached safety.

Isabelle did what she could. She hid the ring of keys away. She summoned the steward and said that she wished to ride, and when he had had a horse saddled for her, she rode out into the countryside until she found a farmer at work in the fields. She asked if he was a Count's man, and when he shook his head, she gave him gold, the horse and this instruction: "Ride to Paris, to the house of the water merchant on the Pont Notre Dame. Say to the men there, 'Isabelle's life depends on your aid.'" She watched the man gallop off. Then she walked back to the castle and told the steward she had been thrown. He sent men in search of the horse.

Once alone in her chamber, Isabelle took the keys from their hiding place to examine them. The shaft of the golden key was stained with blood. Horrified, she rinsed it clean in her own basin before she buckled the ring to the belt at her waist.

When the steward later reported his men's failure to find the horse, he glanced at the keys and remarked, "There is a stain on the golden key, mistress." He gave his sly smile and bowed himself out.

It was true. She rinsed the key again, and it came clean; for safety's sake she scoured it with ashes from the fireplace. Then she put it away in a linen chest.

Within minutes, she reopened the chest. The stain had returned. The key seemed to be bleeding, for the linen beneath it was marred by crimson patches.

Isabelle locked the key into her jewel casket. From time to time during the next days, she cleaned it and laid it away. And as always, the key bled again, leaving crusts upon the shining gems around it.

All through the month that followed, Isabelle maintained her outward composure and, in private, carefully washed the golden key, hoping that the bleeding would stop. As she did so, she silently called her brothers' names. Who knew if the farmer had reached them?

The Count returned at last, clattering through his gate into the courtyard and calling for his wife. She came down to him, her housewife's keys jingling, for it seemed to her that wherever she hid he would find her. When he had embraced her, he asked for the golden key.

"It is not here," said Isabelle.

An expression of infinite, ancient sadness settled onto her husband's face. He took her by the hand and led her into the hall and up the stair to her chamber. He held out his hand. She opened the casket that contained her jewels and gave the Count his bloodstained key.

Then he took her to his long gallery, where the dark men hunted on the walls. Helpless as a captive animal, Isabelle followed. He opened the door to the chamber of his brides, and he said, "The spell was formed, young wife, and none can change it. I must kill the mortal bride, and if the kill is seen, then I must kill the seer. The golden key is the guardian."

"Who made the spell?" asked the wife.

"The old ones made it," said the husband, and would say no more.

Isabelle replied, "My brothers will come to save me, Count."

He shook his head.

"You must dress in your bride clothes, Isabelle, for you have become the bride of death."

"They will save me," she repeated, "and thereby break the spell."

She turned and left him. From her chamber window, she gazed out into the fields of spring, but she saw no horsemen there. Playing for time, she slowly unfastened the keys that still hung at her waist. She unpinned the wimple of the matron, let her hair down in the manner of a bride, dropped her silken gown to the floor and adorned herself in the bridal clothes she had worn when she left her home. Then she stood by the window, waiting.

The steward appeared. "My master summons you to his gallery," he said.

"Tell your master that my brothers are riding to me."

The steward merely gave his secret smile. He went away.

Finally, her husband's step sounded on the stair. His shadow fell across the room.

"Come, Isabelle," he said. "Do not delay the time." She remained by the window, still as a stone. He came closer and tossed the bloodstained key onto the window sill. Then he gave a hoarse gasp. A pair of horsemen were streaking across the fields outside.

He sprang for the door, shouting orders, but he was too late. The castle gates stood open and undefended. The Count met Isabelle's brothers in his courtyard. He screamed horribly as they cut him down. The last she saw of him was a flash of his bloodied body on the paving stones as she rode away behind her eldest brother, heading for home.

The Count in his sepulcher of a castle was among the worst of the beings wrought by spells to walk among humankind. No storyteller could say why he suffered his terrible enchantment. All they could tell was that he was a person made into a predator. He was Death-in-Life, who seduced his victims away from the safety of their kind into his own cold embrace. The enchantment that made him powerful was broken only by his death, and the death was brought about only by humans brave enough to battle him—by Isabelle, caught in the trap but steadily refusing to abandon hope, and by her brothers, who in their loyalty flew to her side and fought the agent of death.

Death was all too close and real in those days. Diseases stalked towns and cities almost unchecked, and (continued on page 109)

EROS·AND·PSYCHE·

The glow of a forbidden lamp revealed to Psyche the true nature of her lover. He was winged Eros — no mortal man but the god of love himself.

Creatures of caprice, powerful and jealous of their power, the old gods of Greece toyed with the lives of men and women, and love and courage and fidelity were all that mortals had to defend themselves To show what strength of heart might do, the Greeks were fond of telling of the sorrows of Psyche and how she bore them

Psyche, a maiden of Caria in Asia Minor, was the very pearl of mortal beauty, tall and pale, dark of hair and bright of eye So lovely was she that she piqued the pride of the goddess Aphrodite, who turned the weapons of magic against her By charms, Aphrodite kept the eligible young mortal men of Caria from the young woman's side And she sent her son Eros to enchant the maiden and make her heart turn toward beasts Once Eros saw Psyche, however, he was himself enchanted She became his object; he set magic in motion to hide the maiden from her parents and from the goddess

Psyche's parents had sent to the oracle of Apollo at Miletus, on the coast, to find why no man offered for their daughter The oracle replied in the voice of Eros rather than Apollo, saying that Psyche was destined not for a youth of her own kind but for a dragon; she must be sacrificed on a high hill that lay near the city People obeyed the oracles in those days Psyche's parents wept, but they took the maiden to the place of sacrifice and left her there among the peaks and cliffs

Alone in the windy waste, high above the roofs of Miletus, the maiden waited for death But all that came was sleep, gentle as an evening tide, and she sank to the ground where she stood

When she awoke, she was in a different place — no arid height but a green valley, watered by silver streams and rimmed by stands of poplar and pine A house stood before her, low and white, with roof tiles glinting gold in the sun 🦋 Its golden door swung open, and the lightest of breezes nudged her toward the entrance 🦋 Within, she found an arcaded courtyard paved with a mosaic of roses, the favorite flower of Eros 🦋 The scent of rose blossoms hung heavy on the air 🦋

No human voice spoke in that house, and no human face appeared 🦋 Invisible hands served food and drink to Psyche on plates fashioned from bronze and in cups that were painted with entwined lovers' figures 🦋 When night fell, invisible arms drew her into a sleeping chamber 🦋 And, invisible in the darkness, a lover came to her 🦋 With his caresses, he taught her joy, but all she heard of his voice was a whisper that said she

Discovery meant loss.
Psyche broke the rule of his
spell, so Eros left her and
fled into the night.

must never see his face 🙟 He left her before dawn 🙟

In this dreamlike enchantment, Psyche lived for months, alone by day except for the airy hands that served her, companioned at night by a lover she never saw 🙟 Even in her pleasure she grew restless and curious 🙟 One night she hid an oil lamp in her chamber, and when her lover turned from her and slept, she lighted it 🙟

Beside her lay a beautiful being—Eros, the most wicked of boys, the most amorous of men 🙟 Folded along his back was not the cloak that had seemed to cover her in the night, but mighty wings glittering with the colors of the dawn 🙟 Psyche's hand trembled; drops of hot and glistening oil

Hoping to win her lover back, Psyche braved the underworld, traveling through tunnels rimed with everlasting frost in search of the land of the dead.

spilled from the lamp and splashed upon Eros' naked skin ❧

Within an instant of the action, she was bereft ❧ Eros sprang up, looked at her in silent reproach for the betrayal of the terms of his spell, and left her ❧ Weeping, she followed ❧ The last she saw of him was the great wings shining in the moonlight ❧

In the morning that followed the long, lonely night, Psyche began her wanderings through the world, walking alone from her valley into the wilderness and crying for Eros ❧ For many days she walked, until at last, all hope spent, she prayed to Aphrodite for Eros' return ❧ The goddess of love heard; mercurial being that she was, she answered ❧ The second part of Psyche's trials began ❧

The goddess demanded that the woman prove her fidelity ❧ She made tasks for Psyche to perform: Psyche must sort the wheat, barley and millet that filled the goddess's granary; she must pluck the golden fleece of fierce rams that grazed in the goddess's meadows ❧ As if nature itself took pity on the mortal maiden, Psyche was given aid ❧ It was said that a tribe of ants appeared to sort the grain for her and that the very hedgerows in the meadows plucked the sheep's fleece with their brambles and offered the wool to Psyche's hands ❧

But the things of nature could not help the woman in her last task ❧ The goddess sent Psyche into the underworld to receive from the Queen of Hades the magical essence of mortal beauty, which Aphrodite demanded as an offering to herself ❧

Armed only with a barley loaf to tempt the dog that guarded Hades' gate and with coins to pay the ferryman who plied Hades' river, Psyche entered a cave and descended into the dark, walking through miles of icy tunnels until she came to the place that the black dog Cerberus

In a pit at the border of the river Styx, Charon the ferryman waited. Psyche gave him gold coins to take her into Hades.

loud on the stones, and called a greeting.

An old woman clothed in black shuffled into the courtyard, nodding and mumbling to herself. She plucked the knight's sleeve and drew him to the house, whispering unintelligibly all the while.

She appeared to be a simpleton, but when she left him at the door of a small chamber in the house, she said quite clearly: "Do not drink the wine. Do not sleep. Do not give up the clothes you wear in this world." Perhaps, thought the knight, she was mad.

The room he entered was cold and almost bare; at a long oak table stood a man with silver hair. He was a tall, fine-looking man, but he was bent and ill, and his voice trembled when he spoke.

"You have come for the venture," the man said.

The knight sighed, for he had been long at war and he was weary of ventures. He had come for a bed. His training held good, however. He could not in honor refuse such a challenge.

"What is the venture, lord?" he asked.

"It is to save my lineage," replied his host. "The daughters of this house are under an enchantment. Each night they disappear and will not say where; each morning they return with their clothes in rags. Each day they grow nearer death, and my house dies with them, as you see. Yet I cannot find the key that will set them free. The venture is to find where they go and shut the door that they have opened."

"Has no one followed them?"

"Three young men have tried. They failed, and I slew them for the failure. Those are the terms of the venture."

"If young men failed, it is folly for an old man to try," the knight observed.

"You refuse it?"

"I accept it."

The host nodded and called a name. Reappearing instantly at her master's summons, the black-robed serving woman led the knight through corridors thick with dust, past empty, shuttered rooms, up a steep stair and into the dormitory shared by the daughters of the house.

This was a long, high chamber overflowing with objects and people. Six enormous curtained beds concealed one wall; chests and stools lay randomly about the room. And scattered helter-skelter on chests and beds and stools and floor were mounds of feminine adornments—silk chemises, stiffened linen cottes for pinching in waists, glittering cauls of golden net for binding hair and veils to cover the cauls, ropes of pearl and chains of silver, gowns of embroidered damask and brocade. Shoes lay everywhere, soft leather court-ladies' slippers of scarlet and blue that were set with winking jewels. Fine as they were, the shoes were grimy and, for the most part, worn to tatters.

Dozing on window seats, stretched out on beds and drooping on stools were the owners of the clothing. The knight counted twelve of them. They had been pretty young women, he supposed, but their lethargy, their bony slenderness, their pallor and the peculiar, transparent quality of their skin gave them the appearance of a tribe of ghosts.

One of them stirred when he cleared his

A forest refuge

Sometimes simple steadfastness aided mortals caught in enchantments, as the tale of Snowdrop shows. She was a maiden as fair as the earliest flower of spring, for which she was named. When her father died, she was given into the care of her stepmother, a Queen and sorceress who possessed a prescient mirror and the amulets and philters of the practiced poisoner. Jealous of the maiden and unwilling to reveal it, the Queen sent Snowdrop into the forest with a huntsman, ordering him to murder her.

But he was her first savior. Loath to kill, he simply abandoned the maid. She wandered alone in the wood until she came upon a tidy hut, and there she found refuge. This was the home of tiny forest people, hunters and woodsmen as old and gnarled as the trees they lived among. Charmed by her fairness, they took her in.

But the Queen had her magic mirror, and it showed that Snowdrop lived. Taking the shape of an old peddler woman, the sorceress traveled to the forest hut and offered the maiden ripe apples. Snowdrop took one; she bit into the flesh and dropped to the ground in a trance, for the apple was a deathlike charm.

The Queen, however, had not understood the fidelity of the little woodsmen, who found Snowdrop as still as death yet flushed with the bloom of life. Unable to rouse her, those rough folk built her a coffin of glass and watched over it faithfully, year after year.

Their vigil ended only when a young lord, hunting in that forest, found the crystal tomb and the maiden who lay there. He opened the glass and gathered Snowdrop into his arms. That was the action that broke the Queen's spell. The poisoned flesh of the apple dropped from Snowdrop's lips, and she lived again — and soon married the Prince. He punished the stepmother, it was said, by forcing her to dance until she died, wearing iron shoes heated until the metal glowed.

throat. At her movement, her sisters awakened, instantly alert to him, although they seemed unsurprised at his presence. They watched with pale eyes while she offered him a bath and fresh clothing, as was the custom in great houses in those days. When the knight refused, they twittered and whispered among themselves. Unnerved, he let himself be led to a corner where a sleeping pallet lay concealed by a curtain. The maiden left him there for a moment, then reappeared with a silver wine cup. When he shook his head at it, hectic color stained her white face. In a shaking voice, she hissed, "It is commanded that you drink."

"In a moment," he said. "When I lie down for sleep." She turned away. He emptied the wine into his tunic, where it seeped dankly along his skin. Then he wrapped himself in his cloak, lay down and closed his eyes.

For an hour or more, the knight lay on his pallet, listening to the sounds outside the curtain — the rustling of fabric, the clink of jewelry and the constant, fluttering murmurs of the women. From time to time, he heard footsteps approach him; he kept his eyes closed, and the watchers went away.

"Poor knight, who drinks the wine of sleep and dies for it," said a voice once.

At last, a sharp clap sounded. In measured pace, feet trod across the floor of the room. The voices of the sisters faded into the distance. When the sounds in the chamber ceased, the knight peered out from his retreat.

A great door stood open in the floor at the foot of the central bed. Even now, the portal was beginning its downward swing. He leaped for it, gained the entrance beneath and dropped down. The door closed seamlessly above his head.

He stood in darkness at the top of a winding stone stair. Laughter echoed from far below. Cautiously, step by narrow step and turn by turn, the knight descended toward the sound. As he progressed, feeling his way along the wall with one hand, the stair grew brighter, until the patterns of the stonework that formed it were clearly defined. He glanced at the wall. The hair on his neck rose as he realized that he could not see his own hand. He looked down. His entire body was invisible.

The knight considered the situation, then shrugged and continued on down the stair. Judging from the weight of the door that closed the entrance, he could not retreat in any case.

The stair debouched at last into a twilit world. Groves of trees spread out before him, shining as if in starlight. Behind the groves, a sheet of water shimmered, and at the center of this lake rose an island palace. Among the trees walked the women he followed. They gave no sign of observing the knight's approach, and he moved quietly among them, marveling.

The sisters had lost their languid pallor and their transparency. They were bright of eye and pink of cheek; their bodies had shed the dry angles of starvation and taken on the curving sheen of healthy young women. It was as if they lived fully only in this place. Chattering and laughing, they strolled along the edge of the lake. Across

In the underworld, an island castle stood. Ghostly ferrymen took maidens
to it, to dance with them there. But once, a living knight went unseen
into the underworld and thwarted the weaving of death's spell.

the water toward them floated a bobbing chain of small, high-prowed boats.

Bemused by the picture and unable to see his own feet, the knight trod on the train of a gown. Its owner turned, looking with wide eyes at the place where he stood. She whispered anxiously to a sister, but the sister merely laughed and quieted her.

Backing away, the knight stationed himself beside a tree to await events. The trunk of the tree was cold; and when he examined the leaves and apples the tree bore, he found that they, too, were icy — not living matter at all. He plucked an apple; heads turned when the entire branch snapped, but none of the women appeared to see him.

The rest was easy. The little boats, piloted by tall men concealed within high-collared black cloaks, arrived at the shore, one for each woman, to carry the sisters across the water. The knight went with them, huddled in the stern of the last boat to launch. Although the pilot complained about the unusual weight, the vessel reached the island safely and beached in the light that streamed from its palace.

The place was a house of death. Within its hall, light glared from no evident source, and wild music soared, played by no musician. The women's pilots shed their cloaks. Livid of flesh and pointed of ear, they were dead men. They swept the sisters into a dance, and as they turned in its figures, the bones of their skulls gleamed through the skin.

Through the hours, they danced without cease. So many puppets, the women hung in their partners' arms, eyes glittering, laughter spiraling shrilly.

And all through the long evening, the knight leaned against a wall and watched unseen. When at last the dead men led their drooping charges out of the hall, he followed, taking with him a silver cup he had found, a token of the journey.

Back the company went across the lake; into the jeweled grove, the women stumbled, with the knight at their heels. Behind them, voices drifted across the water, fading away as they approached the stone staircase. "Soon," said the voices softly, "soon, soon."

When the group neared the top of the stair, the sister at the front clapped her hands once. The door swung up, and one by one, the women stepped into their own world. The old knight came last, and as he ascended through the entrance, his hands and feet appeared to him again: Fully alive, clothed in the garb of the living, he could not be seen among the dead. In his own world, he came into himself again.

At the knight's appearance, the sisters froze where they stood, clustered at the entrance to the underworld. He pushed them back and, with a rough hand, forced down the door. The room trembled as it slammed shut.

"A living man seals this door forever," he said. "It is a foul thing, ladies, to be half in love with death." And he threw down the apple and the silver cup that he had taken. Both crumbled and faded to dust upon the floor.

The venture was won. The door to the underworld, where the sisters had been lured and where their lives ebbed night by

night, was closed forever. Health was restored to the maidens and to their house. Rewarded by their father with lands and gold, the knight married the eldest of the daughters, and the marriage was a fruitful one—a repudiation of death.

Bow the door to the underworld had been opened in the first place and what enchantment had originally caught the maidens, the storytellers never said. They told only that it was shut by a wandering knight—not a young and dashing lord but a battle-scarred veteran who, in spite of his age and weariness, had the courage to face the challenge of a spell and the intelligence to avoid its pitfalls and undo its charm.

The knight's tale was not unique. In the end, it seemed, the best of the human character was sufficient to defeat magic and drive back the dark.

Kindness, perhaps, was the most effective weapon of all, as a story from the chronicles of King Arthur tells:

The tale began with a challenge to the King himself. It happened that during a stag hunt the King left his people to stalk a buck alone. From thicket to thicket he followed the quarry, and at length, he flushed it in the midst of a deep and silent glade, where heavy trees surrounded him, blocking out sight and sound of his companions. He brought the buck down with a single bowshot.

At that moment, a stranger strode out of the shadows of the wood—a knight, fully armored and armed.

"Well met, King," said the knight. "This wood is my territory. You have violated it, and your life is forfeit."

Unshaken, King Arthur examined the stranger for some moments in silence. And then the King said, "How are you styled, knight?"

"I am called the Son of the Summer's Day."

"Then let me tell you, sir, that you are armed and I am not. If you slay me as I stand, your honor will die. But I will strike a bargain with you. In return for my life, I will grant you what you wish."

"Very well, King," said the knight. "Here are my terms, then. You and I shall part now. You shall return here unarmed and alone, this day twelvemonth, and when you return, you will bring me the answer to a question that I have: 'What is it that women desire?' If you cannot find the answer, then you forfeit your life." And the stranger vanished among the trees without a further word.

Arthur set about the business of butchering the stag he had shot, all the while puzzling over the encounter. His life, it seemed, depended on a trivial riddle, asked by a being who was certainly a creature of the other world. But he was not yet done with otherworldly folk. When he had finished the work and marked the place for his huntsmen, he set out through the wood and was once again accosted.

A woman rose, it seemed, out of the ground mist. She was dressed in silk and mounted on a pretty palfrey, but her appearance was so grotesquely ugly that Arthur's heart contracted with pity. Squat as a barrel, she was red of face and lumpy with warts. Crooked teeth protruded over

her wide lips, and yellow matter crusted her red-veined eyes.

"Lady, good day," said the King.

"God prosper you, King," she replied briskly. "Dame Ragnell is my name. I have the answer to the Son of Summer's riddle. Only I have it. My word can save your life, and for a price, I will give you that word."

"What do you wish?"

"That if I ransom you with wisdom, you give me the knight Gawain for a husband."

This was preposterous. Gawain then was the foremost of the King's warriors, unmatched in courage and courtesy, invincible in battle and gracious at court. He was beloved by his companions. He was no man to mate with a fairy crone. Arthur told the woman this, as kindly as he could.

Dame Ragnell shrugged her massive shoulders. "Even an owl must have a mate, and Gawain is the one I choose. When the time of your trial is near, King, I shall come to your court and hear your answer." She turned the little palfrey abruptly, and in a moment, she had disappeared.

For some months, Arthur said nothing about his bizarre meetings in the wood. As the trial drew near, however, and it became clear that he might indeed lose his life to the knight called the Son of Summer, he told his council about the affair. The reaction among them was horrified amusement—at the silliness of the riddle, at the thought of Gawain matched to a hag. But Gawain himself silenced them.

"I will wed the lady, and so tell her," he said. Nothing could shake him. The laughter of his fellows he ignored; the protests of the King he answered by saying that few marriages were happy ones, and that this marriage was better than the death of the King by magic.

The appointed year drew to its close. Dame Ragnell appeared at court, as she had promised. She was received with contempt from the courtiers and grave courtesy from Gawain. He did not flinch when she stroked at his sleeve with knotted hands; he escorted her to the King, slowing his long stride to her rolling waddle. When he had left her with Arthur, one of his fellow knights spat and said, "That is a foul creature, Gawain."

"You must not speak to me of her that way," said Gawain gently. And indeed, no one of Arthur's people dared to speak ill of Dame Ragnell after that.

What she gave the King for the riddle's answer neither one would say. It was the right one, however. Arthur returned from his meeting with the Son of Summer unharmed. That affair was over.

Now the price was paid. Into Arthur's great hall at Carlisle, Sir Gawain led Dame Ragnell, who shuffled along beside him, mumbling and snuffling and cackling to herself. Before the courtiers, he pledged his troth to her, and not a sign did he give that she did not please him, then or throughout the feast that followed, during which the crone tore greedily at her food with long, dirt-rimmed nails and swallowed with loud and liquid gulps. Apparently oblivious to this, Gawain spoke kindly to his wife throughout the meal, and he shared her meat-flecked goblet.

She listened to him for the most part in silence, being occupied with eating. At

The unwinding of one spell began this way: When King Arthur slew a stag on forbidden land, the beast's protector demanded payment—the answer to a riddle or Arthur's life.

She who solved the riddle that saved King Arthur was a repulsive crone.
For her fee, she demanded the hand of Sir Gawain, Arthur's matchless
knight. Gawain, loyal to his King and generous of heart, paid the price.

The hag Gawain married was no hag at all, but the fairest of maidens transformed by magic. By his unfailing courtesy, Gawain fulfilled the spell's terms to free her, and his reward was happiness of a measure few mortals ever knew.

last she leaned back on the bench, her red face shining with grease. Looking along the table at the people of Arthur's court, she said thickly, "For your sake, Gawain, I would be a beautiful woman, for you have such good will." She gave a hoarse chuckle, then, and swayed where she sat.

But Gawain, constant in courtesy, only smiled. Then he rose and helped Dame Ragnell from her place. He gave the crone his arm and led her past the courtiers, out of the hall and to the bridal chamber.

When they were alone there, she eyed her young husband suspiciously and said, "You must fulfill the bargain now. Bedding is the wife's right, and I ask it of you."

"Indeed, lady, I am your true husband." He turned from her to unbuckle his sword.

When he turned back, the crone was gone. Beside the bed a woman stood, slender as a candle flame. A cloud of black hair curled around this maiden's sweet face, and her dark eyes sparkled at him.

He dropped the sword and belt to the floor. "What are you?" he whispered.

She replied with a laugh, "Your wife, surely, Gawain."

While he stared, she continued, "I lie under an enchantment. And the choice of its terms is yours: I can be as you see me when we are alone and a crone when anyone is by. Or I can be beautiful in the eyes of the court and a crone when I am here with you. Choose, then, husband."

"Why, lady," said Gawain, "this is a sad choice. I must lose honor in the eyes of the court or pleasure in love."

"So you must," replied Dame Ragnell.

The young husband thought a moment and then shook his head. "My dear, you must do as you wish. I give the choice to you — and gladly, with my heart."

Dame Ragnell held out her arms to him and said, "Now you have answered the terms of the spell that chained me. My fate was to live as a crone until the greatest knight in Britain married me and gave me sovereignty of choice. I am your true lady, Gawain, and this is the body that I always shall wear." Then she put out the light.

When morning came and sunlight filled the chamber, Gawain propped himself on his elbow and gazed at his wife until she opened her eyes and smiled at him.

"The riddle that the Son of Summer made the King," he said. "What was it?"

"He asked what women most desire."

"And the answer?"

"Sovereignty over men," said Dame Ragnell with a laugh.

Dame Ragnell lived with Gawain for five years and bore him his only son — Gingalin, who grew to be a warrior as strong as his father. The woman's beauty never faded, but — as if the children of the elder races could not survive long among mortals — she died very young. Gawain mourned her all his life.

Loyalty to his King and his own unswerving kindness delivered Gawain's lady from the spell that bound her. And tales of this kind were common once. As men and women slowly came to learn, they had strong defenses against the lingering spells and bindings of the elder age. Those defenses were the courage, strength and love that lay within the human heart.

A Spell-Shackled Devotion

Famed was the valor of the Fianna, that brotherhood of warriors who served as guardians of spell-haunted Ireland, and among the Fianna, none was so highhearted as Diarmuid, son of Donn. Courageous and skilled in battle, he was a sweet singer besides. So merry and generous was his nature that, as the chroniclers said, "all women loved him." Not only mortal women: Diarmuid was the champion of several Princesses of the Side. Stories of his adventures among that ancient fairy race tell of spells broken and evils overcome, but as so often was the case when humans partook of magic, the accounts are wreathed in sadness.

It happened once, for instance, that although Diarmuid's gentleness brought him the brightest of pleasures, his very humanity prevented him from keeping them as his own. The tale began in winter, when snow veiled the Irish hills. During the bitter-cold days, the men of the Fianna hunted stags across the countryside; at night, they gathered in the small hunting lodges that were scattered throughout the forests.

Late one night, well after the men had wrapped themselves in their long cloaks and settled down beside the dying fire to sleep, the door of their lodge flew open with a crash that shook the walls, letting in a blast of cold and snow. The sleepers leaped at once to

On a bitter winter's night, a hag of loathsome aspect burst into a hunting lodge of the warriors of Ireland and begged for shelter.

their feet, reaching for their knives. Even in a time of peace, these warriors were as alert to danger as cats.

But no enemy threatened. In the open door stood a beggar woman. She was a rag-wrapped crone. Her hair was stiff with grime and grease, and rheumy eyes stared from her pockmarked face. A rank smell of dirt and ordure drifted from her tattered clothing into the warm room. She whined for shelter.

The men's leader, whose name was Finn, gave a crack of laughter and threw down his weapon. In distaste, he pulled his cloak around him and turned away, although among the Irish, a stranger, no matter how lowly, was protected by the rules of hospitality. Finn's son joined him, and his son's companions, too.

Only Diarmuid hesitated. Seeing this, the hag redoubled her shrill complaints. At last he said, kindly enough, "Enter, mother. It is the hearth guest's right."

"Keep her on your side of the fire then, Diarmuid," said Finn, but he made no further comment. Diarmuid removed his own cloak, wrapped the woman in it, and lay down beside her at the hearth.

The men muttered drowsily, and someone gave a low laugh, but the old woman lay still. After a few moments, the company drifted back into sleep, and there was no sound in the smoky chamber except the breathing of the men and the occasional whispering of the coals as they settled.

The warriors awoke to the sweet scent of flowers. Beside Diarmuid, there lay a woman, and she was no filthy hag. Rosy with sleep, she stretched and gazed at the men, and sunlight seemed to gather in her hair and sparkle in her eyes.

Finn rose slowly to his feet. "Why, lady, how came you here?" he said.

The lady smiled. "I am a woman of the

Transformed by the kindness of the warrior Diarmuid, the fairy woman took him for her heart's companion. She had learned to love him.

127

Side," she said. "I was condemned by my enemies to wander as a hag until the charity of one man should set me free." And she put her hand in Diarmuid's.

What followed was magic. The woman sang in the strange tongue of her race, and as she sang, the snow cover melted and the trees grew green. A fortress rose on the hillside where the Fianna had hunted, its gray stone walls springing silently from the grass. As the walls grew, shadows and then solid shapes—of splendid hounds and golden-bridled horses, of bards and harpers and serving people—emerged within them and began to move as living things.

It was a palace for Diarmuid, made by her fairy arts. Entranced, he followed her to it, leaving behind his companions of the Fianna. He lived in the palace with his new-found lady for many months, and the chroniclers say that his time with her was one of perfect happiness.

But he marred that happiness himself, through his own quick tongue, and he lost the lady. She could not bear to speak of the long years she had wandered through the wind and weather on ragbound feet, shunned by every living thing. She begged Diarmuid not to talk of that time because of the pain it gave her, and he promised he would not. But in a moment of irritation such as comes to any couple, he snapped at her, "If you remembered the way you were, a stray crone I took in from the cold, you would not anger me thus."

She grew pale, and at once he was sorry for the harsh words. But in the weeks that followed, he said them again, and then again. And at the third saying, she left him. She waited until he slept. Weeping, she walked from the fortress and out across the rolling countryside. Behind her, the gallant castle began to crumble.

When his lady fled, Diarmuid followed her to the shores of the sea. A small boat took him down through the waters to her homeland.

When Diarmuid awoke, he found himself lying on the cold, hard ground. His fortress had vanished, and the lady of the Side was gone. With a cry, he rose. He armed himself and followed. Like most of the Fianna, he was an excellent tracker, and it was not long before he found the path his lady had taken.

As Diarmuid strode along that trail, his eyes alert for signs of the woman's passing, he thrice came across jewels, large tearlike drops the color of blood, formed perhaps from his own cruel words. He wrapped the jewels in a white cloth and placed them in the breast of his tunic.

Diarmuid walked west until he came to the sea, wrinkling in a faint breeze. On the shingle lay a boat, a rich little barge with a curving prow, fine enough to carry a prince. Its helmsman nodded and beckoned. Surrendering himself to his adventure, Diarmuid obeyed the gesture.

The barge sped out across the sea with Diarmuid in the bow, where the waves foamed. The water took on the blue of the deep ocean, then cleared and grew translucent as a jewel. In the depths, as in a rock pool, a landscape appeared. Meadows and forests shimmered beneath the racing shadow of the boat. Mountains loomed. A castle crowned a hill, and around it, tiny figures moved. Nearby, on the banks of a shining river, an old woman gathered rushes.

Into this country the barge suddenly plunged, bearing Diarmuid to the bottom of the sea. With a shudder, the little craft came to a halt near the rush gatherer, and the silent helmsman left Diarmuid there.

The old woman told the warrior what he needed to know. This was the kingdom of Under-Wave, she explained. The rushes she was harvesting were to ease the pain of its Princess, who lay dying in the castle on the hill, weakened by spells that had sent her

Reunited with his lover, Diarmuid showed her the jeweled drops that he had found — and joyfully learned that they could save her life.

131

wandering for seven years and by the cruelty of the man who had freed her from the enchantment. The rush gatherer guided Diarmuid to the castle and the tower chamber where the Princess lay.

He stretched out his arms when he saw her, for she was his own true love, whom he had wounded and now had found again. She smiled at him in her sweet way and said faintly, "Each time I thought of you on the journey here, Diarmuid, a drop of blood fell from my heart."

With trembling hands, Diarmuid showed the Princess the three crimson jewels he had found as he walked.

She nodded and said, "Those drops will make me whole again. But I must dissolve them in the golden cup belonging to the King of Magh an Iongan-aidh, the place the common folk call the Plain of Wonder, in the west. That country is bordered by a river where wind and water go awry. You cannot sail across it, Diarmuid, nor can you swim. And even if you could, I would still die, for no man has ever taken the cup from the King."

But Diarmuid had not found his lady to lose her so easily. "I will find the cup for you, my heart," was all he said. And he left her.

He journeyed westward alone and within two days reached the river that marked the border of Magh an Ionganaidh. The waters had a life of their own, indeed: They flowed south, but even as Diarmuid watched, the current reversed with a white explosion of bubbles and whirlpools and spray; the wind plucked at the waves and sucked them into the air in shimmering columns.

Standing unperturbed on a rock amid the turmoil was a stranger, a tall man, slender in the way of some elves. He was dressed and cloaked in red; even his skin had a ruddy tinge, and his eyes gleamed with flame.

Mighty in battle, Diarmuid slew every warrior who tried to keep him from the golden cup whose magic would restore the health of his lady.

"You will be Diarmuid, son of Donn," he said, and his high, rather light voice sounded clearly above the roar of water.

"I am he," Diarmuid replied. "I wish to cross to Magh an Ionganaidh."

"A brave man," the elf commented, and he gave a glittering smile. "I know your task, Diarmuid, and I can carry you across these waters, but I warn you that mortals fare ill on the Plain of Wonder."

"Nevertheless, I will go there."

In a sudden motion, the elf leaned forward, seeming to stretch to the thinness of a curl of smoke. His hand coiled tendril-like around Diarmuid's ankle. Then, as easily as a man might lift a small child, he raised the Irish warrior to his shoulder and carried him across the roiling waters.

He set Diarmuid on the bank and said, "Fare forward, voyager, and fare well." Before Diarmuid could speak a word of thanks or question, the elf had vanished from view. But the reedy voice spoke again from the air. "I can follow you, Diarmuid. I know you go to save a life. But I cannot aid you now."

So Diarmuid strode forward, onto the barren Plain of Wonder, and by the night of that same day, he stood before the fortress of its King. The gate was bolted, and the walls loomed high above the plain. Diarmuid flung back his head and shouted a challenge: the King's cup of healing for himself, or warriors to defend it.

The answer he got was warriors. They burst through the gate in a pack, screaming their battle cries, their spears at the ready. Straight toward Diarmuid they came. With slingstones, he brought the vanguard down. With his broadsword, he battled the survivors. He fought with the wild fury of his kind, and in the end he stood alone on the plain, surrounded by a moaning cadre of dead and

An elfin guide appeared to Diarmuid, and with a warning, the fiery creature showed the way to a spring that gave forth healing waters.

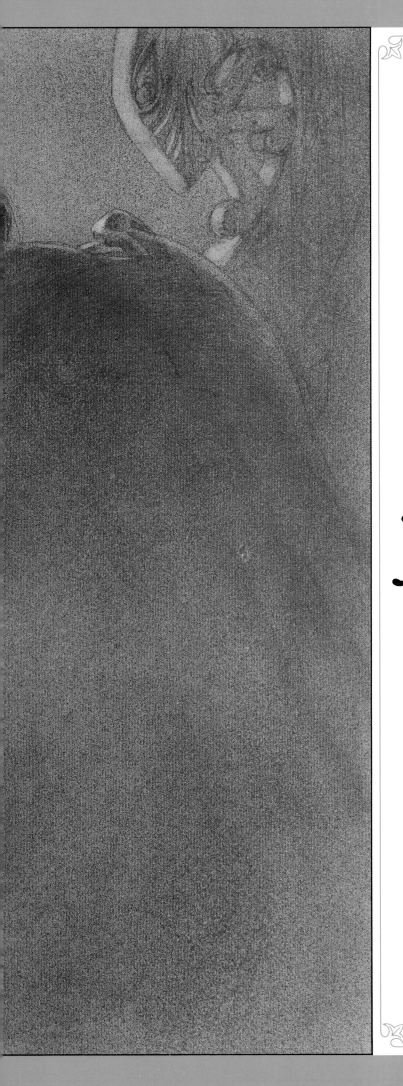

dying men. He wiped his sword blade on the grass and sheathed it.

Then the gate of the fortress swung slowly open. An old man stood in the archway, gazing gravely at Diarmuid. In his hands he bore a golden cup, fretted with starlike jewels that winked in the reddening sun.

"Who is it that kills my finest men?" the old man said.

"I am Diarmuid, son of Donn, and a man of the Fianna of Ireland."

"Then I have heard your name. And more, I have heard it prophesied that you would slay the flower of my warriors. What is it you would have?"

"The cup of healing that you bear," said Diarmuid. And, advancing, the old King gave him the cup and turned and disappeared into his fortress. The gates slammed shut behind him. Without even a glance at the bodies of his enemies, Diarmuid set off.

At the river that bordered Magh an Ionganaidh, the elvish stranger awaited him, as if, invisible, he had been leading the way. "Well, Diarmuid," he said. "It seems that you are determined to give your lady life."

"That is so. And it is not you who will stop me now," Diarmuid replied.

"Oh, I have no wish to stop you," said the elf. "I will give you the wherewithal to heal the lady, and I will help you in the task. But in the healing you will lose her."

"Why?" said Diarmuid.

"Because her kind cannot stay among mortals. Think of the harm that you did before. Would you restore her life only to take it again with careless words?"

Diarmuid bent his head. Then he nodded, and followed where his curious guide led him. The man took him to a small spring and bade him fill the cup with its waters.

"Give her three draughts to drink," said

While Diarmuid watched, his lady drank, and as she drank, her health came to her. But in the same moment, his heart grew cold.

the guide. "Before each draught, drop into the cup a jewel of her heart's blood that you have. When she has drunk, she will be healed. But you will no longer love her, and when she looks at you, she will know it. When you have finished the task, leave us and return to your own kind."

Diarmuid's eyes filled with tears, but he went on his way, through the bordering river and across the fields of Under-Wave to the tower where his lady waited.

She brightened when she saw him, and Diarmuid's heart contracted at her beauty and sweetness. He brought forth the cup he had carried so carefully, and into its water he dropped one blood-red jewel.

"Drink, my heart," he said, and while he watched, his lady drank. Twice more she drank, and when she had drained the golden cup and a wave of delicate rose bloomed once more in her cheek, she looked up into Diarmuid's eyes.

In her pretty face, Diarmuid read at once what his lady saw before her: a mortal man, battle-weary and a little coarse, who gazed at her with indifference and, indeed, impatience. Just as the elf had said, the love had drained from his heart.

She said, "It seems you will leave us." Her voice was cool and filled with the calm wisdom of the fairy people.

"Lady, we must part," he replied.

She nodded and gestured toward the window. From the sky of that world, quivering with watery reflections, a barge floated down toward the hills of the kingdom of Under-Wave. The boat and its silent helmsman had come to take Diarmuid home. He never saw his lady again, although he traveled many times upon the sea. Diarmuid had ceased to love, but he never forgot how he had loved, in a world that was foreign to his own.

Up through the sea waves Diarmuid sailed in an enchanted vessel, back to his own world and his own kind, far from the Princess he had loved.

Picture Credits

The sources for the illustrations in this book are shown below. When it is known, the name of the artist precedes the source of the picture.

Cover: Sir Edward Burne-Jones (detail), courtesy The National Trust, London. 1-5: Artwork by Alicia Austin. 6: Artwork by Julek Heller. 7: Border artwork by Alicia Austin. 9: Howard Pyle, private collection, courtesy Delaware Art Museum and Charles Scribner's Sons; border artwork by Alicia Austin. 10, 11: Border artwork by Alicia Austin. 12: John Duncan, courtesy City of Edinburgh Art Centre, photographed by Sean Hudson, Edinburgh. 14: Border artwork by Alicia Austin. 15, 16: Sir Edward Burne-Jones (detail), courtesy Birmingham Museum and Art Gallery, Birmingham. 17: Border artwork by Alicia Austin. 18, 19: Artwork by John Howe. 21: Edmund Dulac, copyright Geraldine M. Anderson,

from *Sinbad the Sailor and Other Stories from the Arabian Nights*, Hodder and Stoughton, 1914, courtesy Mary Evans Picture Library, London. 23: Border artwork by Alicia Austin. 24, 25: Artwork by Matt Mahurin. 26, 27: Border artwork by Alicia Austin. 28-49: Artwork by Matt Mahurin. 50: John Duncan (detail), courtesy Dundee Art Galleries and Museums, Dundee. 51, 53: Border artwork by Alicia Austin. 54, 55: Artwork by John Howe. 56-59: Artwork by John Collier. 60: Anthony Frederick Augustus Sandys (detail), courtesy Birmingham Museum and Art Gallery, Birmingham. 61: Border artwork by Alicia Austin. 62, 63: Artwork by John Collier. 64, 65: Border artwork by Alicia Austin. 66, 67: Artwork by John Collier. 69-73: Artwork by Donna Neary. 74-87: Artwork by Roberto Innocenti. 88: Artwork by Yvonne Gilbert. 89: Border artwork by Alicia Austin. 91, 92: Artwork by

Yvonne Gilbert. 93: Arthur Rackham, from *Fairy Tales of the Brothers Grimm*, Constable and Co. Ltd., 1909, by permission of Barbara Edwards, courtesy Mary Evans Picture Library, London. 94, 95: Border artwork by Alicia Austin. 96-100: Artwork by Matt Mahurin. 103-108: Illustrations by Sir Edward Burne-Jones engraved on wood by William Morris, from *William Morris: The Story of Cupid and Psyche*, Cambridge and London, 1974, copyright the Society of Antiquaries, by permission of Clover Hill Editions. 111: Artwork by Matt Mahurin. 112, 113: Artwork by Julek Heller. 114, 115: Artwork by Julek Heller; border artwork by Alicia Austin. 116, 117: Border artwork by Alicia Austin. 118-121: Artwork by Michael Hague. 122: Artwork by Michael Hague; border artwork by Alicia Austin. 124-139: Artwork by John Howe. 144: Artwork by Alicia Austin.

Bibliography

Aldington, Richard, and Delano Ames, transl., *New Larousse Encyclopedia of Mythology*. London: The Hamlyn Publishing Group, 1974.

Apuleius, *The Golden Ass*. Transl. by Jack Lindsay. Bloomington, Indiana: Indiana University Press, 1962.

Bloch, Chayim, *The Golem: Legends of the Ghetto of Prague*. Transl. by Harry Schneiderman. Vienna, Austria: Privately published, 1925.

Briggs, Katharine:
An Encyclopedia of Fairies: Hobgoblins, Brownies, Bogies, and Other Supernatural Creatures. New York: Pantheon Books, 1976.
The Personnel of Fairyland. Detroit: Singing Tree Press, 1971.

Bulfinch, Thomas:
Bulfinch's Mythology. New York: The Modern Library, no date.
Myths of Greece and Rome. Compiled by Bryan Holme. New York: Penguin Books, 1981.*

Burton, Richard F., transl., *Tales from the Arabian Nights*. Ed. by David Shumaker. New York: Avenel Books, 1978.

Canby, Thomas Y., "The Rat: Lapdog of the Devil." *The National Geographic Magazine*, July 1977.

Cavendish, Richard, *King Arthur & the Grail: The Arthurian Legends and their Meaning*. New York: Taplinger, 1979.*

Cavendish, Richard, ed., *Man, Myth & Magic*. 11 vols. New York: Marshall Cavendish, 1983.

Cole, Joanna, *Best-Loved Folktales of*

the World. New York: Doubleday, 1982.

Cooper, J. C., *Fairy Tales: Allegories of the Inner Life*. Wellingborough, England: The Aquarian Press, 1983.

Daniels, Cora Linn, and C. M. Stevans, eds., *Encyclopaedia of Superstitions, Folklore, and the Occult Sciences of the World*. Vols. 1, 2 and 3. Detroit: Gale Research, 1971 (reprint of 1903 edition).

Encyclopaedia Judaica. Jerusalem: Keter Publishing House, 1973.

Evans, C. S., *Sleeping Beauty*. New York: Dover Publications, 1976 (reprint of 1920 edition).

Evans, Joan, ed., *The Flowering of the Middle Ages*. New York: Bonanza Books, 1985.

Folkard, Richard, Jr., *Plant-Lore, Leg-*

ends, and Lyrics. London: Sampson Low, Marston, Searle, and Rivington, 1884.

Ford, Patrick K., transl., *The Mabinogi and Other Medieval Welsh Tales.* Berkeley: University of California Press, 1977.*

Gallant, Roy A., *The Constellations: How They Came to Be.* New York: Four Winds Press, 1979.

Gibson, Michael, *Gods, Men & Monsters from the Greek Myths.* London: Peter Lowe, 1977.

Graves, Robert, *The Greek Myths.* Vols. 1 and 2. New York: Penguin Books, 1983.

Green, Roger Lancelyn, *King Arthur and His Knights of the Round Table: Newly Re-Told out of the Old Romances.* Harmondsworth, England: Penguin Books, Puffin Books, 1982.

Gregory, Lady, ed. and transl., *Gods and Fighting Men: The Story of the Tuatha De Danaan and of the Fianna of Ireland.* Gerrards Cross, England: Colin Smythe, 1979 (reprint of 1904 edition).*

Grimm, Jacob, *Teutonic Mythology.* Vol. 2. Transl. by James Steven Stallybrass. Gloucester, Massachusetts: Peter Smith, 1976 (reprint of 1883 edition).

Grimm, Jakob Ludwig Karl, and Wilhelm Karl Grimm:
The Complete Grimm's Fairy Tales. Transl. by Margaret Hunt. New York: Pantheon Books, 1972.*
Fairy Tales of the Brothers Grimm. London: Hodder and Stoughton, 1979.
The German Legends of the Brothers Grimm. Vols. 1 and 2. Ed. and transl. by Donald Ward. Philadelphia: Institute for the Study of Human Issues, 1981.
Grimm's Fairy Tales. New York: Viking, 1973.
Sixty Fairy Tales of the Brothers Grimm. Transl. by Alice Lucas. New York: Weathervane Books, 1979.

Guest, Lady Charlotte, transl., *The Mabinogion, from the Welsh of the Llyfr Coch O Hergest (The Red Book of Hergest).* London: Bernard Quaritch, 1877.

Hall, Louis B., transl., *The Knightly Tales of Sir Gawain.* Chicago: Nelson-Hall, 1976.

Hamilton, Edith, *Mythology.* New York: New American Library, 1969.

Hartland, Edwin Sidney, *The Science of Fairy Tales: An Inquiry into Fairy Mythology.* Detroit: Singing Tree Press, 1968 (reprint of 1891 edition).*

Hindley, Geoffrey, ed., *Larousse Encyclopedia of Music.* London: The Hamlyn Publishing Group, 1974.

Housman, Laurence, *Arabian Nights (Stories Told by Scheherazade).* New York: Abaris Books, 1981.

Humble, Richard, *The Explorers* (The Seafarers series). Alexandria, Virginia: Time-Life Books, 1978.

Jacobs, Joseph, *English Fairy Tales.* New York: Dover Publications, 1967 (reprint of 1898 edition).

Joyce, P. W. *A Smaller Social History of Ancient Ireland.* London: Longmans, Green, 1906.

Karr, Phyllis Ann, *The King Arthur Companion.* Privately published, 1983.

Lang, Andrew, ed., *The Blue Fairy Book.* New York: Dover Publications, 1965 (reprint of 1889 edition).

Leach, Maria, ed., *Funk & Wagnalls Standard Dictionary of Folklore, Mythology and Legend.* 2 vols. New York: Funk & Wagnalls, 1949.*

Lehane, Brendan, *The Companion Guide to Ireland.* London: William Collins Sons & Company, 1973.

MacCulloch, J. A., *The Childhood of Fiction: A Study of Folk Tales and Primitive Thought.* London: John Murray, 1905.*

MacCulloch, John Arnott, and Jan Machal, *Celtic, Slavic.* Vol. 3 of *The Mythology of All Races.* New York: Cooper Square, 1964.*

McDermott, Beverly Brodsky, *The Golem: A Jewish Legend.* Philadelphia: J. B. Lippincott, 1976.

Malory, Sir Thomas:
Le Morte D'Arthur. 2 vols. Edited by Janet Cowen. New York: Penguin Books, 1969.
Le Morte Darthur. Edited by R. M. Lumiansky. New York: Charles Scribner's Sons, 1982.*

Morford, Mark P. O., and Robert J. Lenardon, *Classical Mythology.* New York: Longman, 1977.

Mulherin, Jennifer, ed., *Favourite Fairy Tales.* London: Granada Publishing, 1982.

Opie, Iona, and Peter Opie, *The Classic Fairy Tales.* New York: Oxford University Press, 1980.

Ovidius Naso, Publius, *Ovid: Metamorphoses.* Transl. by Rolfe Humphries. Bloomington: Indiana University Press, 1955.*

Perrault, Charles, *Perrault's Fairy Tales.* Transl. by A. E. Johnson. New York: Dover Publications, 1969 (reprint of 1697 edition).

Pyle, Howard:
The Story of the Champions of the Round Table. New York: Dover Publications, 1968 (reprint of 1905 edition).
The Story of King Arthur and His Knights. New York: Charles Scribner's Sons, 1903.

Quiller-Couch, Sir Arthur, *The Sleeping Beauty and Other Fairy Tales from the Old French.* New York: Abaris Books, 1980.

Rees, Alwyn, and Brinley Rees, *Celtic Heritage: Ancient Tradition in Ireland and Wales.* New York: Thames and Hudson, 1961.

Rolleston, T. W.:
The High Deeds of Finn and Other Bardic Romances of Ancient Ireland. New York: Lemma Publishing, 1973.
Myths & Legends of the Celtic Race. London: George G. Harrap, 1911.*

Ross, Anne, *Pagan Celtic Britain: Studies in Iconography and Tradition.*

London: Routledge and Kegan Paul, 1967.

Sanders, Tao Tao Liu, *Dragons, Gods & Spirits from Chinese Mythology*. New York: Schocken Books, 1980.

Saul, George Brandon, *The Shadow of the Three Queens*. Harrisburg, Pennsylvania: The Stackpole Company, 1953.

Saul, George Brandon, transl., *The Wedding of Sir Gawain and Dame Ragnell*. New York: Prentice-Hall, 1934.

Spence, Lewis, *British Fairy Origins*. Wellingborough, England: The Aquarian Press, 1981.

Squire, Charles, *Celtic Myth & Legend, Poetry & Romance*. North Hollywood, California: Newcastle Publishing, 1975.

Steele, Flora Annie, *English Fairy Tales*. New York: Mayflower Books, 1979 (reprint of 1918 edition).

Stephens, James, *Irish Fairy Tales*. New York: Abaris Books, 1978.

Thompson, Stith:
The Folktale. Berkeley: University of California Press, 1977.
Motif-Index of Folk-Literature. Bloomington: Indiana University Press, 1955.

Thompson, Stith, transl. *The Types of the Folktale: A Classification and Bibliography*. Helsinki: Academia Scientiarum Fennica, 1961.*

Weston, Jessie L., *The Legend of Sir Gawain: Studies upon Its Original Scope and Significance*. New York: AMS Press, 1972 (reprint of 1897 edition).

Whitelock, Dorothy, *The Beginnings of English Society*. Harmondsworth, England: Penguin Books, 1981.

Winston, Clara, and Richard Winston, *The Horizon Book of Daily Life in the Middle Ages*. New York: American Heritage, 1975.

Yarwood, Doreen, *European Costume: 4000 Years of Fashion*. New York: Bonanza Books, 1982.

* *Titles marked with an asterisk were especially helpful in the preparation of this volume.*

𝕬cknowledgments

The editors wish to thank the following persons and institutions for their assistance in the preparation of this volume: Ancilla Antonini, Scala, Florence; François Avril, Curator, Département des Manuscrits, Bibliothèque Nationale, Paris; Laure Beaumont, Chief Curator, Cabinet des Estampes, Bibliothèque Nationale, Paris; Clark Evans, Rare Book and Special Collections Division, Library of Congress, Washington, D.C.; Marielise Göpel, Archiv für Kunst und Geschichte, West Berlin; Julian Hartnoll, London; Elizabeth H. Hawkes, Associate Curator, Delaware Art Museum, Wilmington, Delaware; Christine Hofmann, Bayerische Staatsgemäldesammlungen, Munich; Ann Hughey, Potomac, Maryland; Norbert Humburg, Museum of Hameln, Hameln, Germany; Heidi Klein, Bildarchiv Preussischer Kulturbesitz, West Berlin; Roland Klemig, Bildarchiv Preussischer Kulturbesitz, West Berlin; Waltraud von Kries, Westfälisches Landesmuseum für Kunst und Kulturgeschichte, Münster; Kunsthistorisches Institut der Universität, Bonn; Ivan Loskoutoff, Courbevoie, France; Bernd Meier, Kunstbibliothek, West Berlin; Christine Poulson, London; Beatrice Premoli, Museo Nazionale delle Arti e Tradizioni Popolari, Rome; Luisa Ricciarini, Milan; Justin Schiller, New York City; Robert Shields, Rare Book and Special Collections Division, Library of Congress, Washington, D.C.; Tessa Sidey, Assistant Keeper, Birmingham Museum and Art Gallery, Birmingham, England; Clara Young, Keeper of Art, Dundee Art Galleries and Museums, Dundee, Scotland.

Chief Series Consultant

Tristram Potter Coffin, Professor of
English at the University of Pennsylvania, is a leading authority on folklore.
He is the author or editor of numerous
books and more than one hundred articles. His best-known works are *The British Traditional Ballad in North America*, *The
Old Ball Game*, *The Book of Christmas Folklore* and *The Female Hero*.

This volume is one of a series that is based
on myths, legends and folk tales.

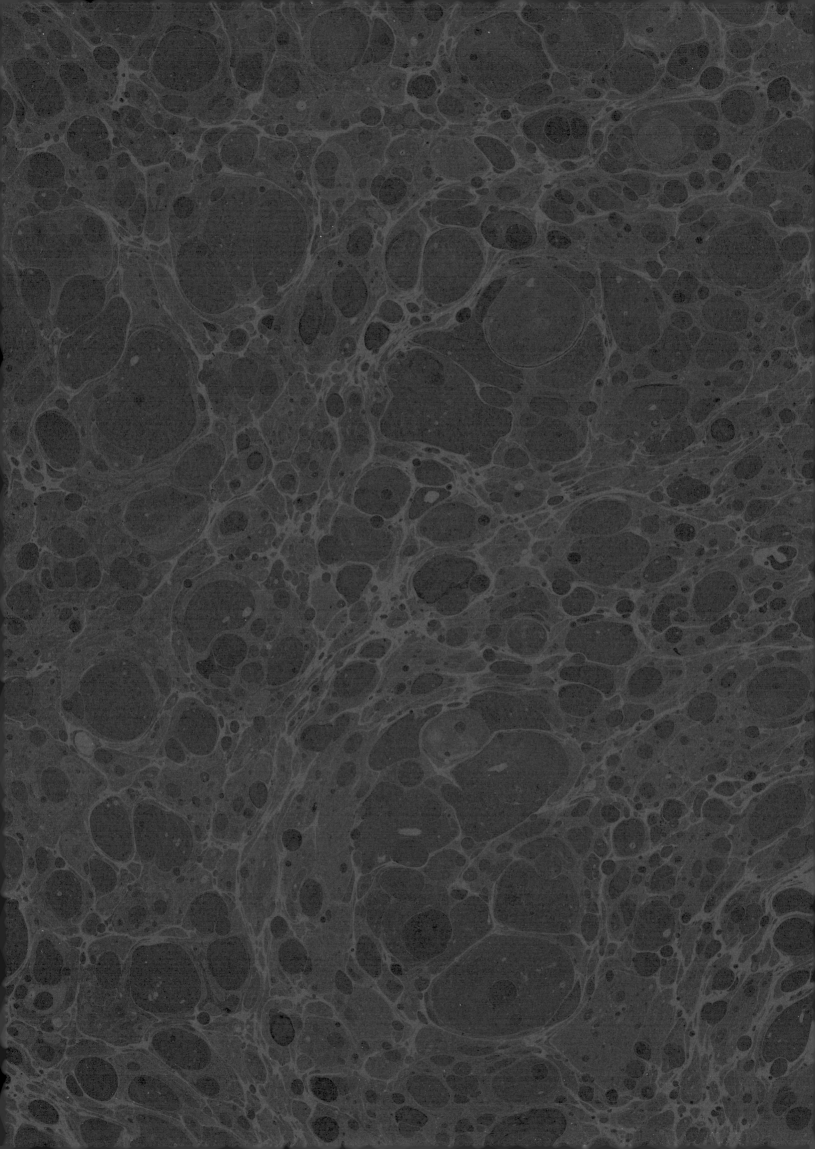